Get ready for... Movers

2nd Edition

OXFORD
UNIVERSITY PRESS

Where do you live?

Words

1 **Listen and read.** 🔊 **1**

Hello, I'm Jack.
Here's a picture of my house, and this is my address. I live at number 38 Swan Street, Littlemore.

Jack Morris,
38 Swan Street,
Littlemore

2 **Listen and point to the numbers. Then write the words.** 🔊 **2**

| fifty | one | hundred | twenty | sixty | eighty |
| forty | seventy | thirty | ninety | ten | |

40
forty

100
_____

10
_____

60
_____

30
_____

80
_____

20
_____

90
_____

50
_____

70
_____

3 **Write the numbers.**

twenty-one forty-nine fifteen sixty-two ninety-four fifty-six

Reading & speaking

1 **Listen, read and find.** 🔊 **3**

Hi! I'm Daisy.
This is my address.
I live in a flat on the fifth floor.
My brother is at home.
He's dressing up.

Daisy Simms,
Flat 5a,
74 Browning Road,
Littlemore

2 **Listen and point to the numbers.**
Draw lines. 🔊 **4**

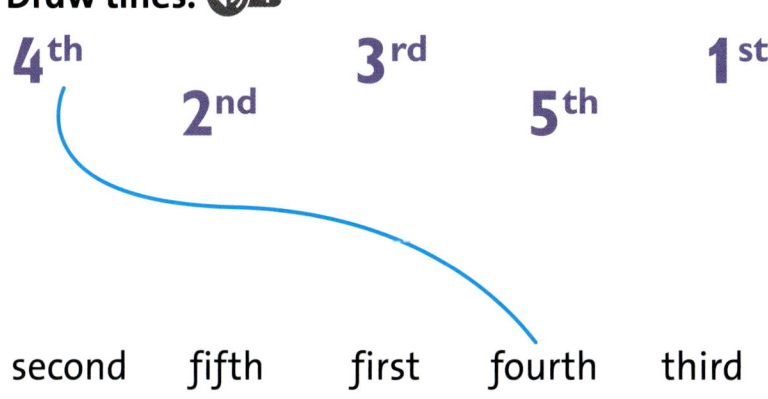

4th   3rd   1st

2nd   5th

second   fifth   first   fourth   third

3 **Complete the sentences.**

1 There are two girls on the ____third____ floor.

2 There's a cat in the __basement__ .

3 There's a television on the _____ floor.

4 There's a woman on the _____ floor.

5 There's a lamp on the _____ floor.

6 There are two men on the _____ floor.

7 There are some toys on the _____ floor.

4 **Find more things in the picture.**
Ask and answer.

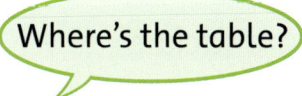

Where's the table?

It's on
the ground floor.

1 At the park

Words

Jack and I like playing in the park.

1 Complete the verbs.

hop skip walk climb ~~laugh~~ roller skate dance cry fish hide

1 l a u g h

2 c _ _ _ _

3 d _ _ _ _ _

4 h _ _ _

5 f _ _ _ _

6 r _ _ _ _ _ _
s _ _ _ _ _

7 s _ _ _

8 c _ _ _ _ _

9 h _ _ _

10 w _ _ _

2 Look and write the colours.

orange pink yellow black ~~green~~ ~~purple~~ brown ~~blue~~ red grey

1 a ___green___ coat

2 a ___purple___ sweater

3 a ___blue___ scarf

4 a pair of _____ socks

5 a pair of _____ trousers

6 a pair of _____ shoes

7 an _____ T-shirt

8 a pair of _____ glasses

9 a _____ jacket

10 a _____ swimsuit

Reading & speaking

1 **Read, look and write the numbers.**

a He's wearing a red sweater.   8

b They're skipping.   ____ and ____

c She's carrying a doll.   ____

d They're fishing.   ____ and ____

e They're wearing blue T-shirts.   ____ and ____

f He's roller skating.   ____

g He's hopping.   ____

h They're wearing glasses.   ____ and ____

2 **Play the game. Say and guess.**

> I'm hopping.

> Are you number five?

> No. I'm carrying a car.

> I know. You're number nine.

3 🎤 **Listen and circle.** 🔊**5** **Ask and answer.**

1 What are you wearing today?

2 What colour are your shoes?

3 Do you wear glasses?   yes   no

Story

1 **Listen and read. Then act.** 🔊 6

2 **Look and write.**

roller skating   tennis   ~~drawing~~   basketball

1 Jack's friend is good at _____ *drawing* _____.

2 The women in the park aren't good at _____.

3 Those girls _____.

4 That man _____.

Language practice

1 **Write the opposites.**

| young | ~~big~~ | short | long |

1

small _____big_____

2

tall _____

3

old _____

4
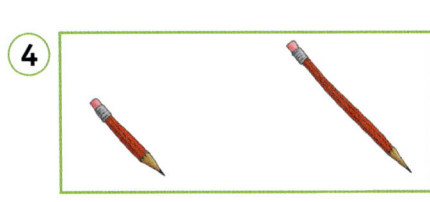
short _____

2 **Look and write.**

| bigger | younger | ~~taller~~ | older | smaller | ~~shorter~~ |

1

The boy _____is shorter than_____ the girl.

The girl _____is taller than_____ the boy.

2

The man _____ the woman.

The woman _____.

3

The green book is _____ the red book.

_____.

3 **Do the speaking activity.** **P** 121

I've got Ben.

I've got Kim.
Kim is older than Ben.
One point for me!

Language practice

1 **Write the colours. Listen and check.**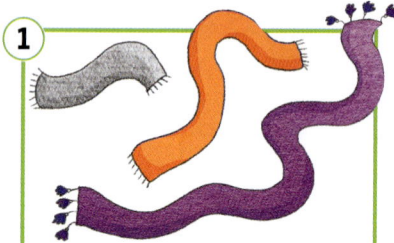

The orange scarf is longer than the _____grey_____ scarf, but the _____ scarf is the longest.

The yellow tree is taller than the _____ tree, but the _____ tree is the tallest.

The blue flower is smaller than the _____ flower, but the _____ flower is the smallest.

2 **Look at the cards and write.** **P 121**

1 _____ is the tallest child.

2 _____ is the shortest boy.

3 _____ is the oldest girl.

4 _____ is the oldest child.

5 _____ is the youngest boy.

6 _____ is the tallest girl.

3 **Find and circle. Write *yes* or *no*.**

In the picture, can you find:

1 a boy who is skipping? ___yes___

2 a girl who is wearing a yellow hat? ___no___

3 a cat that is asleep? _____

4 a man who is wearing glasses? _____

5 a woman who has got a red bag? _____

6 a dog that is brown and white? _____

7 a tree that has got flowers? _____

8 a boy who has got an ice cream? _____

GRAMMAR Superlative adjectives; Relative clauses page 119

Movers practice test

Listen and draw lines. There is one example. 🔊 8

Sally   Jim   Peter   Mary

Jane   Paul   Fred

Movers practice test

Look and read and write.

Examples

The man and the woman are _____ walking _____.

Where's the red car? ___ next to the tree ___

Complete the sentences.

1 The smallest dog is brown and the biggest dog is _____.

2 A girl is playing with a yellow _____.

Answer the questions.

3 What's the girl in the purple coat doing?

_____

4 How many houses are there?

_____

Now write two sentences about the picture.

5 _____

6 _____

Movers practice test

Listening, Part 5

Listen and colour and write. There is one example. 🔊9

2 A busy week

Words

Daisy's got a very busy week.

1 Write the words.

| ride | CD | homework | film | walk | website |
| music | ~~shopping~~ | drive | swim | DVD |

1 go __shopping__

2 do your _____

3 go for a _____

4 go for a _____

5 go for a _____

6 go for a _____ on your bike

7 watch a _____ (or a _____)

8 listen to _____ (or a _____)

9 look at a _____ on the internet

2 Write the verbs.

| email | sail | ~~text~~ | cook | wash | call |

1 __text__ my friend

2 _____ my friend

3 _____ my friend

4 _____ dinner

5 _____ a boat

6 _____ the car

GRAMMAR *like* + verb + *ing*

UNIT 2 WORDS page 113

Reading & speaking

1 **Look, read and answer the questions.**

	Paul	Jim	Fred	Peter
(making paper boat)	✗	✓	✓	✗
(swimming)	✗	✓	✗	✓
(sailing)	✓	✗	✓	✓
(cooking)	✓	✗	✗	✓
(washing car)	✗	✓	✗	✓
(calling)	✓	✓	✓	✗
(emailing)	✓	✗	✓	✓

1 He likes calling his friends, but he doesn't like emailing them. He loves making things.

What's his name? _____ Jim _____

2 He likes going sailing and going for a swim, but he doesn't like making things.

What's his name? _____

3 He likes calling and emailing his friends. He loves cooking dinner, but he doesn't like washing the car.

What's his name? _____

4 He doesn't like cooking dinner or washing the car, but he loves making things and calling his friends.

What's his name? _____

2 **Write about you.**

I like _____ and _____,

but I don't like _____ or _____.

3 🎤 **Listen and circle.** 🔊10 **Ask and answer.**

1 Do you like shopping?   yes   no

2 Who cooks dinner in your house?   mum   dad   me

3 Do you like making things?   yes   no

4 How often do you go swimming?   never   every week   every day

Story

1 **Listen and read. Then act.**

1 Do you like cooking, Jack?

Yes, I do. I like making cakes. How about you?

2 I love cooking. I always cook dinner in our house.

Really?

3 Daisy! Shall I make pasta for dinner?

That's a good idea – yes, please. I love pasta.

4 Your mum's cooking dinner, Daisy. You don't always cook dinner!

Well, no. But I often cook dinner on Thursdays!

2 **Find and circle. Write the days of the week and answer the question.**

FASATURDAYMDMONDAYKOSUNDAYULWEDNESDAYEBRPFRIDAYSHOSTUESDAYEATHURSDAYC

M onday

Tu _____

W _____

T _____

F _____

Sa _____

S _____

Always use a capital letter for the days of the week!

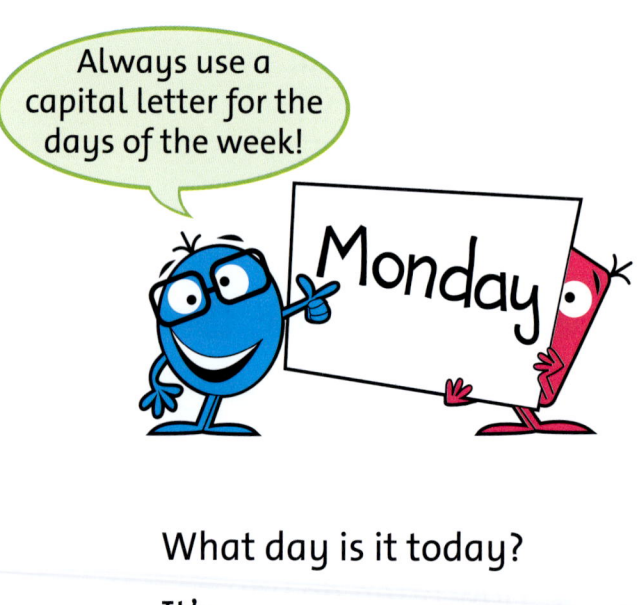

Monday

What day is it today?

It's _____.

Language practice

1 **Do the speaking activity.** **P** 122 and 123

When does Sue play tennis?

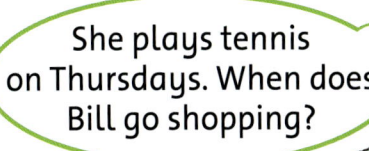

She plays tennis on Thursdays. When does Bill go shopping?

He goes shopping on Mondays.

2 **Write these adverbs in your own language.**
Circle the adverbs that are in the story on page 14.

✗ never _____

✓ sometimes _____

✓ often _____

✓ always _____

3 **Listen. Tick (✓) three things that Jack does at the weekend.** 🔊 12

4 **Write four true sentences about you.**

I	never	text my friends	at the weekend.
	sometimes	do my homework	on Saturdays.
	often	watch TV	on Sundays.
	always	cook dinner	on Wednesdays.

1 _____

2 _____

3 _____

4 _____

Language practice

1 **Read the questions and the answers. Draw lines.**

1 Shall I make pasta for dinner?　　　　　　a No, thanks. It isn't dirty.

2 Shall I wash the car?　　　　　　　　　　b No! It's too big!

3 Shall I draw a picture?　　　　　　　　　c Yes. Draw a house.

4 Shall I climb that tree?　　　　　　　　　d Yes, please. I love pasta.

2 **Complete the rhyme. Listen and say.** 🔊 13

> skating　~~brown~~　like　about　you　too　blue

I've got brown eyes, brown eyes, brown eyes.
I've got brown eyes. How about you?

I've got blue eyes, blue eyes, blue eyes.
Yours are [1] _____brown_____, but mine are [2] _____!

I wear glasses, glasses, glasses.
I wear glasses. What about [3] _____?

Look at my glasses, glasses, glasses.
I wear glasses, just [4] _____ you!

I like tennis, football, baseball.
I like sport – so how [5] _____ you?

I like [6] _____, swimming, running.
You like sport and I do [7] _____!

GRAMMAR *Shall I ...?; How/What about ...?* page 119

Reading & Writing, Part 2

Read the text and choose the best answer.
Paul is talking to his friend Fred.

Example

Paul: Are you in the kitchen, Fred?

Fred: A It's here.
      (B) Yes, I'm here.
      C Yes, you are.

Questions

1 **Paul:** What are you doing?

   Fred: A He emails his friends.
          B I'm doing my
             homework.
          C It's a computer.

2 **Paul:** Is that your computer?

   Fred: A No, it's my dad's.
          B Yes, they are.
          C It's on the table.

3 **Paul:** Do you like swimming?

   Fred: A Yes, you like it.
          B No, it doesn't.
          C Yes, I love it!

4 **Paul:** Would you like to go for
         a swim at the weekend?

   Fred: A Yes, I'd like that.
          B Yes, they like it.
          C Yes, I can.

5 **Paul:** Let's go on Saturday.

   Fred: A No, it's Sunday.
          B I'm going there.
          C All right.

6 **Paul:** Shall I text you on
         Friday?

   Fred: A I went to school on
             Friday.
          B No. Call me.
          C No, you're not.

Movers practice test

Listen and tick (✓) the box. There is one example. 🔊14

Where does Lily live?

A  ✓ B  C

1 Who does she live with?

A  B  C

2 What does Lily do in the park?

A  B  C

3 Which girl is Lily's friend?

A  B  C

4 What does Lily do in the evenings?

A  B  C

Movers practice test

Read the text and the example. Choose the right words and write them on the lines.

Weekends

Do you go to school on Saturdays? What about Sundays?

Example Children don't go to school _____ *at* _____ the weekend.

What do they do on those days? Lots of children

1 _____ their homework. Many children have

2 hobbies too. Some children like _____ tennis

3 or going _____ football practice.

When they are at home, they can listen to music, watch

4 films _____ read books and e-books. There are

5 lots of things to do when you _____ at school!

Example	to	in	(at)
1	do	doing	are
2	play	plays	playing
3	to	for	on
4	but	or	can
5	aren't	isn't	don't

3 In the town

Words

1 Look and complete the crossword. Find the word.

bus station   shopping centre   playground   circus   ~~hospital~~
funfair   car park   market   square   supermarket   train station   town

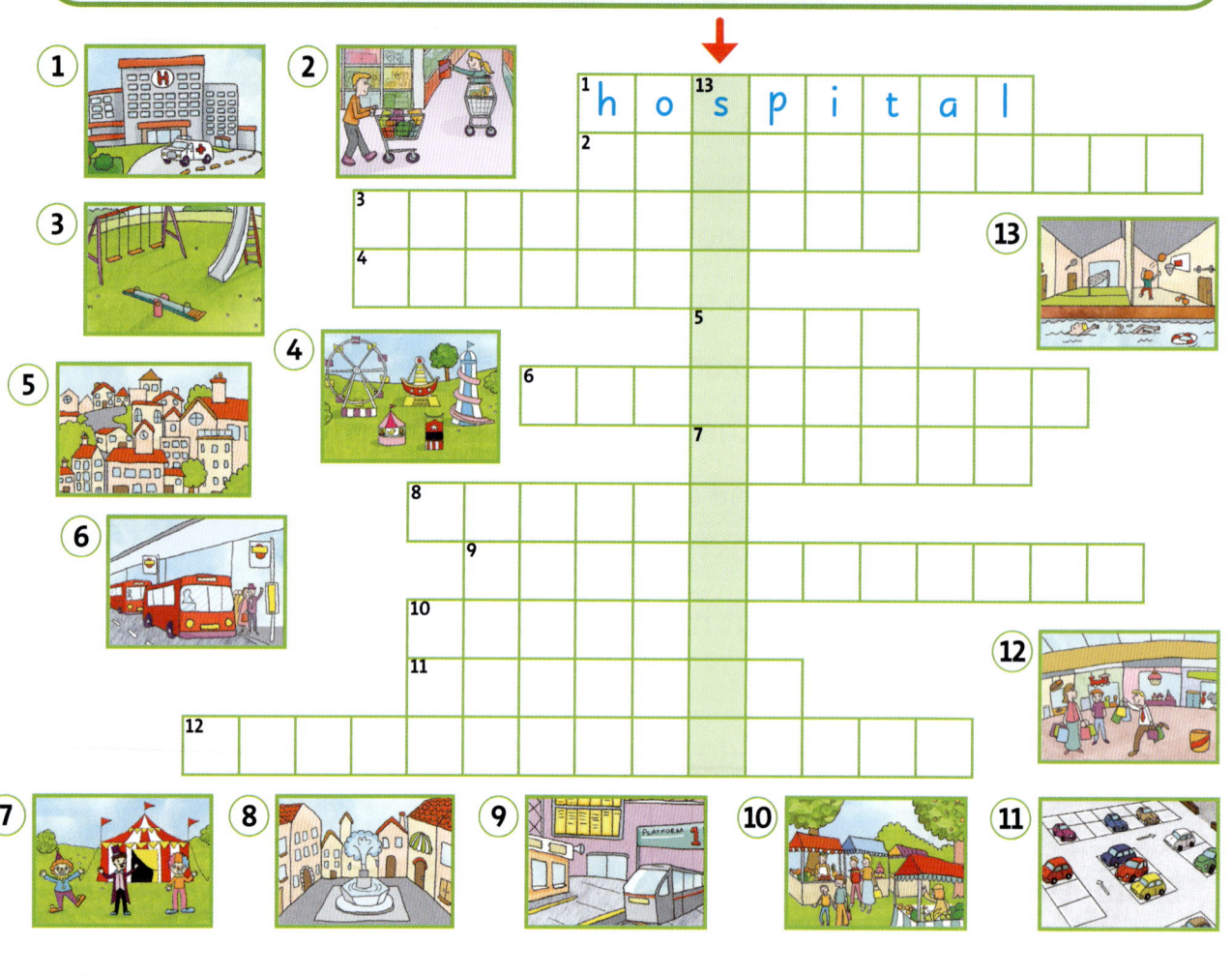

¹ h o s ³ p i t a l

What's 13? It's a _____.

2 Write the prepositions.

near   below   opposite   above

1 Daisy is _____ Jack.

2 Daisy is _____ Jack.

3 Daisy is _____ Jack.

4 Daisy is _____ Jack.

Reading & speaking

1 **Read questions and answers about a town centre. Draw lines.**

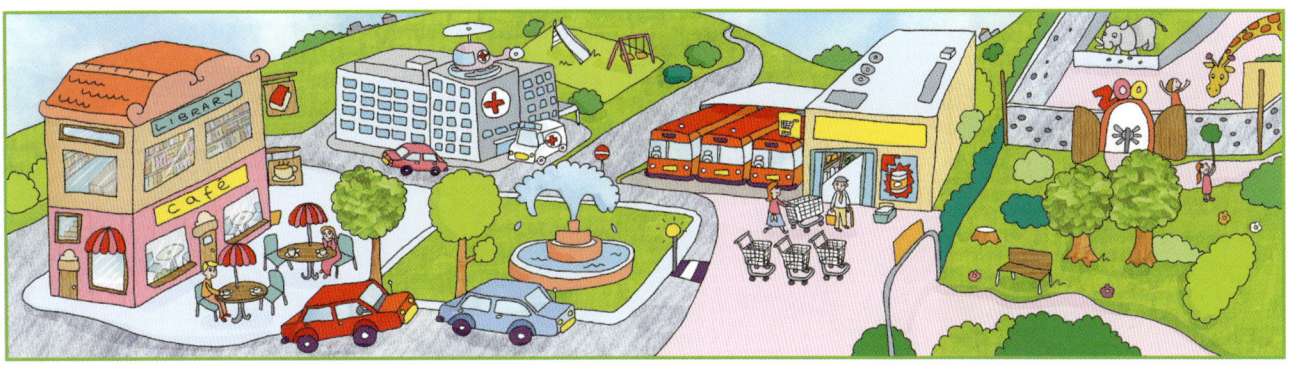

1 Where's the café?		**a** It's next to the bus station.
2 Where's the helicopter?		**b** It's behind the park.
3 Where's the supermarket?		**c** It's below the library.
4 Where's the zoo?		**d** It's on the roof of the hospital.
5 Where's the hospital?		**e** It's near the hospital.
6 Where's the playground?		**f** It's opposite the bus station.

2 **Read and draw the things in the picture.**

There are two birds flying above the library.

There is a man near the bus station.

A woman is standing between the trees in the square.

There is a dog in the park.

3 **Look at the picture. Ask and answer.**

> Excuse me. Where's the park, please?

> It's in front of the zoo.

4 **Listen and circle.** 🔊 15 **Ask and answer.**

1 Is there a library in your town?	yes	no
2 Do you often go to cafés?	yes	no
3 What's your favourite shop called?	Tony's Toys	Book Fun

Story

1 Listen and read. Then act. 🔊16

1 What day is it today?
It's Tuesday. We've got English first.
Oh. Yes, you're right.

2 Last Saturday, I went to the library to do my homework.
Right.
After that, I went to the toy shop.
Oh, why?

3 To buy a present. Do you want to see it?
OK. Who's it for?

4 It's for you. Happy birthday!
Thank you, Jack! I was sad, but I'm happy now!

2 Look and write. What did Jack do on Saturday?

> have a drink   buy a present   catch a bus
> listen to a band   ~~do his homework~~

1 **1** First he went to the l<u>ibrary</u> to <u>do his homework</u>.

2 Then he went to the t_____ sh_____ to _____.

3 **3** After that he went to the c_____ to _____.

4 Then he went to the p_____ to _____.

5 **5** Then he went to the b_____ s_____ to _____.

GRAMMAR **The past simple (*went*) page 119;**
Infinitive of purpose

UNIT 3 WORDS page 113

Language practice

1 **What did they do on Saturday? Look and write the names.**

1 She went to the library, and she went to the town centre.
   She didn't go to the sports centre.   Name: _____

2 She didn't go to the playground. She went to the supermarket,
   and she went to the sports centre.   Name: _____

3 She went to the playground, and she went to the sports centre.
   She didn't go to the supermarket.   Name: _____

2 **Complete the questions and answers.**

1 Where did Clare go on Saturday afternoon?

   She went to the _____ *town centre* _____.

2 Where did Zoe go on Saturday morning?

   She _____.

3 Where did Anna and Zoe go on Saturday afternoon?

   They _____.

4 Where did _____ go on _____?

   She went to the library.

3 **Do the speaking activity.** P 124

GRAMMAR The past simple (*went*) page 119

Language practice

1 **Look at the pictures of Jack and Daisy. Write sentences.**

hot   cold   ~~happy~~   ~~sad~~   afraid   surprised   wet   tired

1 She _was_ happy.

2 _They_ were s_ad_.

3 _She_ was s_____.

4 _____ were h_____.

5 _____ _____ t_____.

6 _____ _____ a_____.

7 _____ _____ w_____.

8 _____ _____ c_____.

Look!

I / He / She / It **was** …
You / We / They **were** …

2 **Look, read and draw lines.**

 When Daisy hops,   he is often afraid.

 When Daisy's mum is happy,   her sister is happy.

 When Daisy makes a cake,   her dad laughs.

 When Daisy's brother sees a big dog,   she always sings.

 When Daisy listens to her favourite pop star,   she sometimes cries!

GRAMMAR The past simple (*was/were*) page 119; *when* clause (present tenses)

UNIT 3 WORDS page 113

Movers practice test

Look and read. Choose the correct words and write them on the lines.

a library

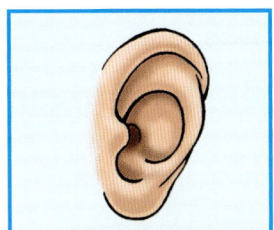
an ear

a table

a playground

a phone

a supermarket

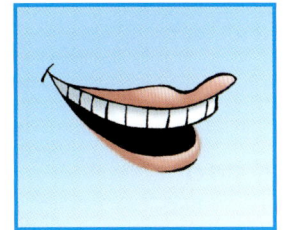
a mouth

an armchair

Example

This is in your house and it has got four legs.
When you eat your dinner, you put food on it.   _____a table_____

Questions

1 You smile, eat and talk with this.
  It is on your face.   _____

2 There are lots of books here. You can read
  them here or you can read them at home.   _____

3 This is in the living room and you can sit on it.
  It is smaller than a sofa.   _____

4 This is part of your body. You listen with it.   _____

5 This is a very big shop. You can buy food here.   _____

Listening, Part 3

Peter is telling Mrs Green about his family and friends and where they went today. Where did each person go?

Listen and write a letter in each box. There is one example.

 Charlie `E`

 his dad ☐

 his brother ☐

Jim ☐

 his sister ☐

Lily ☐

A

B

C

D

E

F

G

H

Movers practice test

Look at the pictures and read the story. Write some words to complete the sentences about the story. You can use 1, 2 or 3 words.
There are two examples.

All about me

My name is Grace. I have got a dog called Ben. He is small, but he is good at running. I live in a flat with three bedrooms. My bedroom is the smallest. There is a computer in my room, but I don't enjoy playing games on it. I like writing emails or using apps. On Saturdays, I sometimes go to the library in the morning. There are lots of good books and CDs at the library.

Examples

Grace's dog is good _____ _at running_ _____.

There are __three__ bedrooms in Grace's flat.

Questions

1   Grace has got the _____ bedroom.

2   Grace enjoys writing _____.

3   She sometimes goes _____ on Saturday mornings.

Yesterday was Wednesday. It was my birthday. After lunch, I went to the sports centre with my family and some friends. The sports centre is huge. You can play hockey there. I like to practise hockey every weekend. It is is my favourite sport! After that, we went to a café near the park.

4   Yesterday was Grace's _____.

5   You can _____ at the sports centre.

6   They went to a café that is _____.

4 At home

Words

1 **Find the things and draw lines.**

bat   blanket   laptop   comic   cage   shower   towel

map of the world   helmet   plant   toothpaste   toothbrush

2 **Find the shapes and complete the sentences.**

Can you find something round ⬤ on the bedroom wall?
Yes, it's a _____.

Can you find something square 🟩 on the bathroom wall?
Yes, it's a _____.

3 **Can you name more things in the picture? Write the words.**

In Jack's bedroom	In the bathroom
a desk	a bath

Reading & speaking

1 **Read and write *A* or *B*.**

A

B

1 There are two chairs.   *A*

2 There's a blue blanket on the bed.   ____

3 There are two pictures above the bed.   ____

4 There's a bat on the desk.   ____

5 There aren't any books.   ____

6 There's a plant with red flowers.   ____

7 There isn't a lamp.   ____

8 There are two CDs next to the laptop.   ____

9 There isn't a TV.   ____

10 There's a comic under the bed.   ____

We use *any* in these negative sentences and questions.

There aren't **any** books.
Are there **any** comics?

2 **Choose a picture in Activity 1 and play a memory game.**

Is there a lamp?

Yes, there is.

Are there any chairs?

No, there aren't.

3 **Complete the sentences about your own bedroom.**

There's _____.   There isn't _____.

There are _____.   There aren't any _____.

4  **Listen and circle. 🔊18 Ask and answer.**

1 Do you live in a house or a flat?   house   flat

2 How many bedrooms are there?   2   3   4

3 Do you listen to music in your bedroom?   yes   no

Story

1 **Listen and read. Then act.** 🔊19

2 **Look and write the colours.**

inside

outside

upstairs

downstairs

1 The _brown_ cupboard is upstairs, but the _____ cupboard is downstairs.

2 The _____ chair is outside, but the _____ chair is inside.

3 The _____ kite is inside, but the _____ kite is outside.

4 The _____ clock is downstairs, but the _____ clock is upstairs.

UNIT 4 **WORDS** page 114

Language practice

1 **Complete the rhyme. Listen and say.** 🔊 20

> picked up   looked   danced   dropped   shouted
> walked   smiled   shopped   planted   ~~skipped~~

I sk _ipped_____ and I da _____ and I sh _____ at my brother.

I pl _____ some flowers and I sm _____ at my mother.

I p _____ a ball and I dr _____ it on the ground.

I w _____ and I sh _____ and I l _____ around the town.

2 **Look. Choose and complete the sentences.**

> listen / listened   close / closed   ~~call / called~~   fish / fished
> watch / watched   sail / sailed   ~~email / emailed~~   open / opened

He didn't __email__ his friend.
He __called__ him.

They didn't _____ to music.
They _____ a film.

He didn't _____ the door.
He _____ it.

In the past simple, we use the infinitive for negative sentences and questions.

She didn't _____.
She _____.

GRAMMAR   The past simple (regular verbs) page 119

Language practice

1 Write the verbs in the past simple. What did Daisy do this morning? Listen and tick (✓) the pictures. 🔊 21

> ~~woke up~~ ate made got took
> had got up rode bought saw

wake up
woke up ✓

get up
_____

eat an apple
_____

have breakfast
_____

buy an ice cream
_____

see Jack
_____

take some photos
_____

ride her bike
_____

get dressed
_____

make a cake
_____

2 Do the speaking activity. **P** 125

What did she do?

What did she see?

Is it number four?

She went sailing.

She saw a snake.

That's right!

GRAMMAR The past simple (irregular verbs) · **UNIT 4 WORDS** page 115

Movers practice test

Look and read and write.

Examples

There is a clock above the _____ door _____.

What colour is the cat that's outside the café? _____ grey _____

Complete the sentences.

1 The man with a wet coat has got black _____.

2 There are three cakes on the biggest _____.

Answer the questions.

3 How many people are there in the café?

_____

4 What is the small boy doing?

_____

Now write two sentences about the picture.

5 _____

6 _____

Listen and write. There is one example. 🔊22

Shopping

How many shops?   5

1   Favourite shop: the _____ shop

2   Where: in _____ Street

3   Phone number: _____

4   Bought: two _____

5   and a _____

Movers practice test

Read the story. Choose a word from the box. Write the correct words next to numbers 1–5. There is one example.

My name is Jane. Last weekend I __walked__ to the zoo with my mum and my brother. First, we looked at the giraffes. One of the giraffes looked at me, and I think it (**1**) _____ ! My favourite animal was a very long snake. It was beautiful, and I took a (**2**) _____. My brother was afraid, but I wasn't. We had lunch in the (**3**) _____. I ate a (**4**) _____, and I drank some water. After that we went to the shop. I (**5**) _____ a comic book about animals. There are lots of funny stories in it.

Example

walked

bought

café

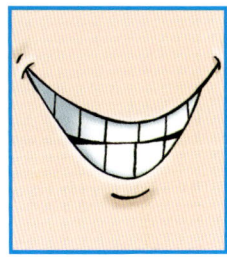

smiled

burger

hippo

rode

photo

(6) Now choose the best name for the story. Tick (✓) one box.

A book about animals ☐

Jane's day at the zoo ☐

Lunch in a café ☐

Revision 1

1 **Look and answer the questions.**

1 What is under the bed? _____ *a shoe* _____

2 What is below the map? _____

3 What is between the mat and the shoe? _____

4 What is behind the chair? _____

5 What is inside the cage? _____

6 What is next to the cage? _____

7 What is on the mat? _____

8 What is above the plant? _____

2 **Read and draw the things in the picture.**

There is a doll in front of the chair.

There is a laptop on the table next to the bed.

There is a helmet on the floor near the window.

There is a picture above the bed.

REVISION 1 WORDS pages 112–114

3 **Read and colour the hats.**

1 The boy with a wet shoe is wearing a green hat.

2 The woman who is riding a horse has got a black hat.

3 The girl who is buying a banana is wearing a purple hat.

4 The man with the yellow sweater is wearing a brown hat.

5 The boy with a bag has got an orange hat.

6 The girl who is hopping is wearing a green hat.

7 The man who is wearing a scarf has got a red hat.

8 The woman who is listening to music has got a blue hat.

4 **Complete the sentences.**

1 The children who are wearing green hats are near the

_____.

2 The people with scarves are in the _____.

3 The woman with a blue hat is sitting outside the

_____.

5 Look and read. Draw lines.

have breakfast

have a shower

go for a swim

go to school

get dressed

send an email

go shopping

wake up

have a bath

get up

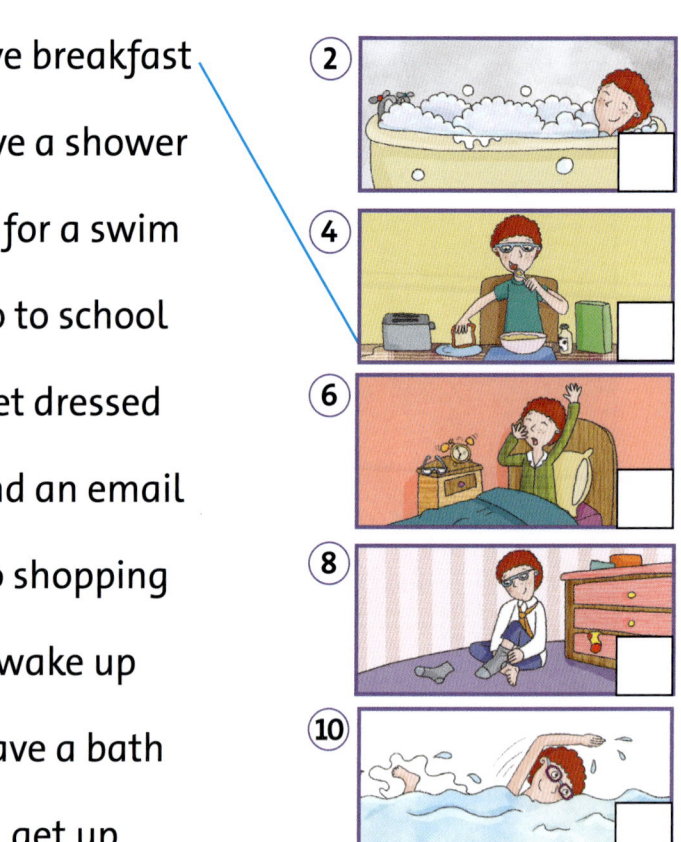

6 What did you do this morning? Put a tick (✓) or cross (✗) next to each picture in Activity 5. Then write six sentences.

I had breakfast.

I didn't have breakfast.

_____.

_____.

_____.

_____.

_____.

_____.

7 What do you do at the weekend? Complete the sentences. Use phrases from Activity 1.

I always _____.

I often _____.

I sometimes _____.

I never _____.

I always get up!

1 Circle five differences and complete the sentences. Listen and check. 🔊 23

A

B

In Picture A, the pencils are _____ **on** _____ the table,

but in Picture B they're _____ it.

This clock is _____ ,

but this one is _____ .

In Picture A, the boy's reading a _____ ,

but in Picture B he's reading a _____ .

The girl's sweater is _____ ,

but here her sweater is _____ .

There's a _____ in this picture.

but there's a _____ in this picture.

2 Look at the pictures. Circle the words that you think will be in the story.

a   b 1   c   d

talking   bat   baseball   afraid   tree   hospital   playing

park   swimming   ball   happy   tennis

3 Listen and order the pictures in Activity 2. 🔊 24   Tell the story.

5 Lets go on holiday!

Words

1 **Write the numbers.**

I'm on holiday with my family.

ticket ☐   wave ☐ 1   cinema ☐   stairs ☐   seat ☐

lift ☐   sea ☐   balcony ☐   beach ☐   swimming pool ☐

2 **Look at the picture in Activity 1 and draw lines.**

1 A woman

2 A boy

3 A girl

4 A man

5 Two children

a is getting on a motorbike.

b is writing a message in the sand.

c is sitting on a seat.

d are getting off their bikes.

e is getting on a bus.

Reading & speaking

1 **Do you know any American words? Read, then write the British words.**

I love watching **movies** at the cinema!

My dad likes walking up the stairs, but I like going in the **elevator**.

I bought this ice cream at the **store**!

American word	British word
movie	f __ __ __
elevator	l __ __ __
store	sh __ __

2 **Read, look and write *yes* or *no*.**

We're waiting at the bus stop!

① ② ③ ④ ⑤ ⑥ ⑦ ⑧ ⑨ ⑩ ⑪ ⑫ ⑬ ⑭ ⑮ ⑯ ⑰ ⑱ ⑲ ⑳

1 Is the third person a man?   _____yes_____

2 Is the twelfth person a girl?   _____

3 Has the fifth person got a bag?   _____

4 Is the last person carrying a towel?   _____

5 Is the second person wearing a skirt?   _____

6 Has the eleventh person got curly hair?   _____

7 Is the ninth person wearing jeans?   _____

8 Is the eighteenth person a woman?   _____

3 🎤 **Listen and circle.** 🔊25 **Ask and answer.**

1 Did you go on holiday last year?   yes   no

2 Do you like swimming in the sea?   yes   no

3 Has your house or flat got a balcony?   yes   no

Story

1 Listen and read. Then act. 🔊26

2 Read and colour.

1 The hat that Daisy wore on the beach was purple.

2 The ice cream which Daisy's mum ate was green!

3 The bird that Daisy's sister saw was blue.

4 The bag which they took to the beach was orange.

3 Listen and colour more things in the pictures. 🔊27

Language practice

1 Write the numbers. Complete the sentences with the past simple form of the verbs.

See the irregular verb list on page 121.

> sleep   watch   go   swim   play   ~~have~~

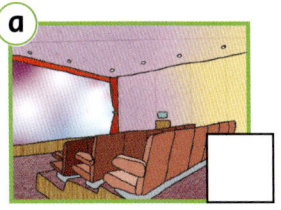
a

b

c   1

d

e

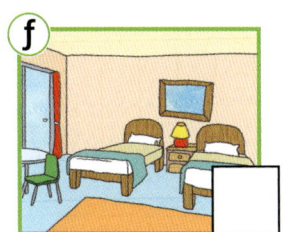
f

1 This is the balcony where Daisy ____had____ breakfast.

2 This is the sports centre where she _____ tennis.

3 This is the town where she _____ shopping.

4 This is the cinema where she _____ three films.

5 This is the room where she _____ at night.

6 This is the swimming pool where she _____ every day.

2 Complete the sentences.

1 A place where people swim is called a _____ swimming pool _____.

2 The room where you sleep is called a _____.

3 A place where people watch films is called a _____.

4 The big shop where you buy food is called a _____.

5 A place where you can do lots of sports is called a _____.

3 Do the speaking activity. **P** 126 and 127

What did you eat in the café?

I ate a cake.

GRAMMAR   Relative clauses with *where* page 119

Unit 4   **43**

Language practice

1 **Write sentences that mean the same.**

1. The girl bought a milkshake for Daisy.
The girl bought ___Daisy a milkshake___.

2. Jack sent an email to Daisy.
Jack sent Daisy _____.

3. Daisy made a sandwich for her brother.
Daisy made her brother _____.

4. Jack told a story to his brother.
Jack told his _____.

5. Daisy showed her picture to Jack.
Daisy _____.

6. Jack gave a present to his mum.
_____.

2 **Complete the rhyme. Listen and say.** 🔊 28

> a chair   a snake   a pear   a story
> some lunch   ~~an ice cream~~   a book   a cake

She bought me ___an ice cream___,
She bought me _____.
I cooked her _____,
And I pulled out _____.

He told them _____,
He made them _____.
They read him _____,
And they showed him _____!

Movers practice test

Listening, Part 1

Listen and draw lines. There is one example. 🔊29

Jim　　　　　　Vicky　　　　　　Jane　　　　　　Charlie

Mary　　　　　　　　　　Fred　　　　　　　　　　Peter

Movers practice test

Reading & Writing, Part 2

Read the text and choose the best answer.

Kim is talking to her friend Anna.

Example

Anna: Where's the cinema?

Kim: A You can
watch films.
B It's a circus.
C It's there.

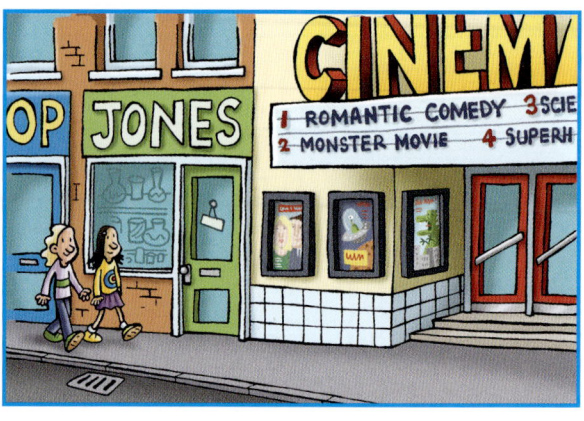

Questions

1 **Anna:** Do you like films?

Kim: A I love them!
B Yes, you do.
C It's great!

2 **Anna:** Do you often watch
DVDs at home?

Kim: A It's a TV.
B Yes, they are.
C Yes, I do.

3 **Anna:** Did you come
here last week?

Kim: A No, it's yesterday.
B No, I was
on holiday.
C Yes, it did.

4 **Anna:** Is your brother
here too?

Kim: A She's here.
B He's at home.
C Yes, he can.

5 **Anna:** Shall I buy the
tickets now?

Kim: A OK.
B Yes, I shall.
C Yes, I've got them.

6 **Anna:** Do you want a milkshake?

Kim: A It's here.
B Yes, it does.
C I'd like that, thanks.

Movers practice test

Listen and tick (✓) the box. There is one example. 🔊30

What clothes did Sally's mum buy yesterday?

A  B 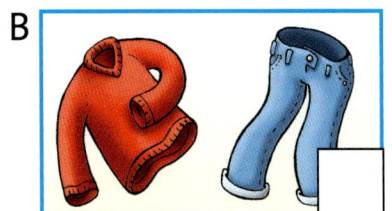 C 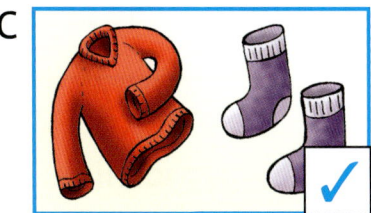 ✓

1 Where did Sally go this morning?

A  B  C

2 Which is Sally's house?

A  B  C

3 What is in her bedroom?

A  B  C

4 What did she do after lunch?

A  B  C

6 My favourite book

Words

1 Number the people, places and things in the picture.

> 1 camera   2 doctor   3 town   4 clown   5 island   6 city
> 7 machine   8 farmer   9 nurse   10 jungle   11 pirate
> 12 treasure   13 village   14 train driver   15 robot   16 cook

2 Write the words in the correct box.

People	Places	Things
doctor	town	camera

UNIT 6 WORDS page 115

Reading & speaking

1 Complete the crossword.

Across →

1 This person works with food in a kitchen.

6 This person works with doctors in a hospital.

7 This is a kind of bag that women often carry.

8 You can take photos and make videos with this.

9 Pirates sometimes find this in stories.

Down ↓

1 This man wears funny clothes. People laugh when they see him.

2 This place is smaller than a town.

3 This person works on a farm.

4 This is a hot place, with lots of trees and animals.

5 You can't drive to this place because it is in the sea.

2 🎤 **Listen and circle.** 🔊³¹ **Ask and answer.**

1 Do you live in a city, a town or a village?   a city   a town   a village

2 Would you like to be a farmer?   yes   no

3 Which do you like best, books or comics?   books   comics

Story

1 Listen and read. Then act. 🔊 32

2 Listen and tick (✓) the box. 🔊 33

1
a  b  c

2
a  b  c

3 Write about a book and draw. Do the speaking activity. P 128

What's your book about?

It's about a girl and her dog.

Is it called *My friend Pat*?

Yes!

Is there a picture on the front?

Yes. There's a picture of a girl and a dog.

Language practice

1 Circle the correct adjectives.

This book is **boring** / easy!

This book is **difficult / famous**!

This book is **terrible / brilliant**!

This book is **exciting / difficult**!

This book is **easy / terrible**!

This book is **famous / boring**!

2 Look. Write *exciting* or *difficult*.

How exciting is it?			
How difficult is it?			

1 Book 1 is more _____exciting_____ than Book 3.

2 Book 2 is more _____ than Book 3.

3 Book 2 is the most _____ book.

4 Book 1 is the most _____ book.

3 Look and say the words. Listen and circle the best kite and the best ball. ◀))34

```
 👍        👍👍       👍👍👍
good  →  better  →  best
 👎        👎👎       👎👎👎
bad   →  worse   →  worst
```

GRAMMAR Comparatives and superlatives page 119

UNIT 6 WORDS page 115

Language practice

1 **Look and complete the sentences.**

1 Paul wants Fred to ___*draw a building*___.

2 Mary is inviting Sue to _____.

3 Ben is asking Jane to _____.

4 Jill wants Tony to _____.

5 Alex is telling Vicky to _____.

2 **Read, look and draw lines.**

1 **One** of the clowns   **a** are wearing red shoes.

2 **Both** of the clowns   **b** are wearing jackets.

3 **One** of the pirates   **c** has got a red nose.

4 **Some** of the pirates   **d** have got red hair.

5 **Most** of the pirates   **e** is eating a banana.

6 **All** of the pirates   **f** are smiling.

3 **Look again and complete the sentences.**

1 ___*One of the clowns*___ has got green hair.

2 _____ have got one leg.

3 _____ are wearing hats.

4 _____ are wearing big shoes.

GRAMMAR   *ask / want / invite* someone to do something page 120

UNIT 6 WORDS   page 115

Look at the pictures and read the story. Write some words to complete the sentences about the story. You can use 1, 2 or 3 words. There are two examples.

Fred's weekend

My name is Fred, and I want to tell you what I did last weekend. I went to see my cousins, Jim and Clare. They live on a farm. It's a nice place, and I love going there. Jim is ten, like me, but Clare is younger than us. On Saturday morning, we went outside. We played in the garden all morning. Then we had lunch in the garden too. We ate chicken and chips.

Examples

Fred's cousins are called _____ Jim and Clare _____.

Fred likes going to the _____ farm _____.

Questions

1 Clare is _____ than Jim and Fred.

2 The children played in _____ on Saturday morning.

3 They had _____ for lunch.

After that, Clare said, 'Please can you take a photo, Fred?' I took a photo, then I played football with Jim. We both love playing football. I scored a goal! Clare didn't play with us. She went to the supermarket with her mum. They bought some meat and fruit for dinner.

4 Clare wanted Fred to _____.

5 Fred and _____ both enjoy playing football.

6 Clare and her mum went to _____ to buy some food.

Movers practice test

Listen and colour and write. There is one example. 🔊 35

Movers practice test

Read the text and the example. Choose the right words and write them on the lines.

Monkeys

Example   Do you like monkeys? Some monkeys are small and some _____ are _____ big. The smallest monkey in the world is about 12 centimetres tall! Most monkeys

1   _____ in the jungle in hot countries,

2   _____ there are monkeys in some cold

3   countries too. All monkeys are good _____ climbing trees. They love playing in the trees with

4   _____ friends. They eat fruit and plants, and

5   they sometimes eat small animals _____.
They love eating bananas!

Example	is	(are)	were
1	lives	living	live
2	or	but	where
3	at	to	for
4	his	our	their
5	too	and	then

7 This is my family

Words

1 Look and write the names.

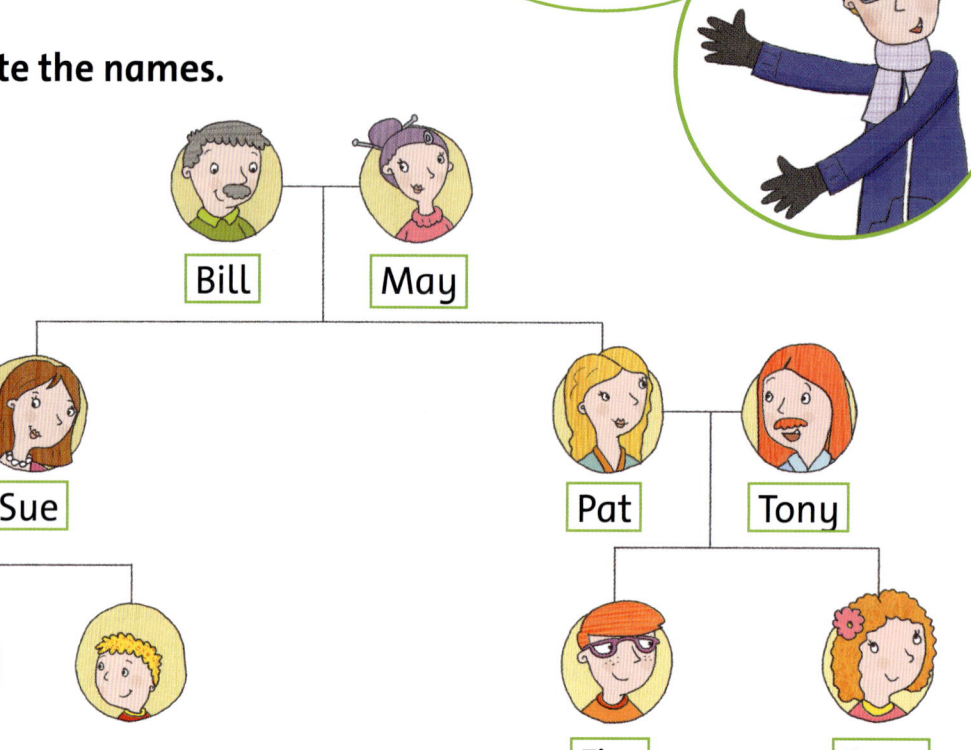

This is Daisy's family tree.

(1) ___Sue___ is Daisy's **mother**, and (2) _____ is Daisy's **father**. They are her **parents**.

(3) _____ is Daisy's **aunt**, and (4) _____ is Daisy's **uncle**.

(5) _____ is Daisy's **grandmother**, and (6) _____ is Daisy's **grandfather**. They are her **grandparents**.

(7) _____ is Daisy's **brother**, and (8) _____ is her **sister**.

(9) _____ and (10) _____ are Daisy's **cousins**.

2 Now look and write the numbers.

1 Alex and Sue have got __one__ **son(s)** and __two__ **daughter(s)**.

2 Pat and Tony have got _____ **child(ren)**.

3 Bill and May have got _____ **grandson(s)** and _____ **granddaughter(s)**.

4 There are _____ **grown-ups** in the picture.
   There are _____ **children** in the picture.

Reading & speaking

1 **Colour the pairs that mean the same.**

| mother | grandpa | dad | grandmother |

| grandma | father | mum | grandfather |

2 **Read, look and write *yes* or *no*. Circle two adjectives that mean the same.**

Has Daisy's father got ...

brown hair? __no__   fair hair? _____

long hair? _____   short hair? _____

curly hair? _____   straight hair? _____

a blonde beard? _____   a red moustache? _____

3 **Listen and draw and colour.** 🔊36 **Listen and draw lines.** 🔊37

① Jack's father

② Jack's uncle

③ Jack's grandfather

④ Jack's cousin

a
Age: 44
Home: house
Work: supermarket

b
Age: 21
Home: flat
Work: café

c
Age: 39
Home: house
Work: hospital

d
Age: 62
Home: flat
Work: library

4 🎤 **Listen and circle.** 🔊38 **Ask and answer.**

1 How many grown-ups live with you?   1   2   3

2 Have you got any brothers or sisters?   yes   no

3 How many cousins have you got?   2   4   6

Story

1 **Listen and read. Then act.** 🔊39

1

Look at that woman! She's riding very quickly!

That's my grandmother.

2

She's 63.

Oh! How old is she?

3

She rides very well!

When did she learn?

Yes, she does. But she couldn't ride a horse when she was young.

4

I learned to ride when I was sixty.

Wow!

2 **Look and complete the sentences with *could* or *couldn't*.**

couldn't ✗ could ✓		age 3	age 4	age 5	age 6	age 7	age 8	age 9
	roller skate	✗	✗	✗	✗	✓	✓	✓
	ride a horse	✗	✗	✗	✗	✗	✓	✓
	swim	✗	✗	✓	✓	✓	✓	✓

1 Daisy ___couldn't___ swim when she was three.

2 She _____ roller skate when she was seven.

3 She _____ ride a horse when she was six.

4 She _____ roller skate when she was four.

5 She _____ swim when she was five.

6 She _____ ride a horse when she was eight.

GRAMMAR *could / couldn't* (past) page 120

UNIT 7 WORDS page 116

Language practice

1 Complete the table about you. Do the speaking activity. **P** 129

> Could you ride a bike when you were three?

> No, I couldn't.

> Could you swim when you were seven?

> Yes, I could.

2 Write four true sentences.

I could _____ when I was _____.

I couldn't _____ when I was _____.

I _____

_____

3 Read, look and write the numbers. Complete the sentences with *could* or *couldn't*.

1 Jack _could_ write when he was three, but he _could_ draw a circle.

2 Jack _____ dance, but his friends _____.

3 Jack's parents _____ see lots of houses, but Jack _____.

4 Jack _____ build a den, but Jack's brother _____!

5 Jack _____ go for a bike ride, but his brother _____.

6 Jack _____ climb the tree, but he _____ climb down!

GRAMMAR *could / couldn't (past)* page 120

Language practice

1 **Write the adjectives, then draw lines to the opposites.**

loud   bad   ~~quiet~~   slow   good   quick

quiet

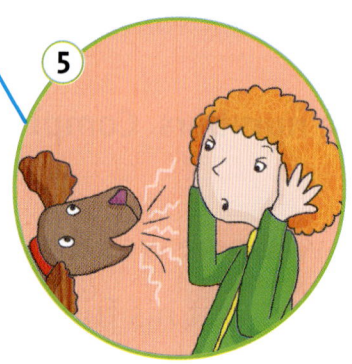

2 **Read, look and draw lines.**

Be careful! The adverb of *good* is *well*.

1 Daisy's parents

2 Daisy's grandfather

3 Daisy and Jack

4 The horses

5 Daisy's grandmother

6 Daisy's sister

a are singing loudly.

b are running quickly.

c is talking quietly.

d are playing badminton well.

e is walking slowly.

f is roller skating badly.

UNIT 7 WORDS   page 116

Movers practice test

Kim is telling Mr Day about her family and what they bought today. What did each person buy?

Listen and write a letter in each box. There is one example. 🔊40

 her aunt **D**

 her mother ☐

her uncle ☐

her grandfather ☐

 her cousin ☐

her sister ☐

A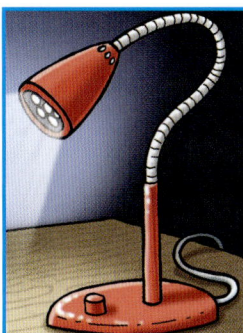

B

C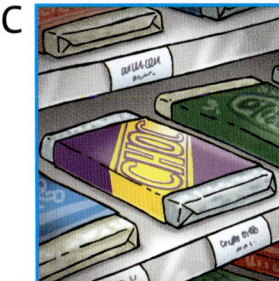

D

E

F

G

H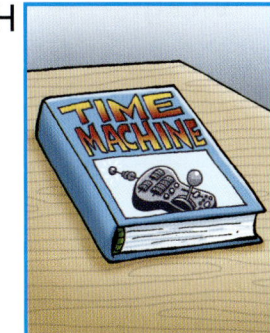

Reading & Writing, Part 2

Read the text and choose the best answer.

Vicky is talking to her friend Jane.

Examples

Jane: What are you doing, Vicky? Are you washing the car?

Vicky: A It's here.
B I'm in the garden.
C Yes, it's very dirty.

Questions

1 Jane: Shall I help you?

Vicky: A Yes, please.
B No, they can't.
C OK, it's a car.

2 Jane: Have you got any water?

Vicky: A No, it's wet.
B Yes, there are.
C Yes, I have. It's here.

3 Jane: Is it your dad's car?

Vicky: A No, it's my mum's.
B No, he doesn't.
C Yes, it was.

4 Jane: Do you like helping your parents?

Vicky: A Yes, they do.
B Yes, sometimes.
C It helps them.

5 Jane: Would you like to have a car like this?

Vicky: A Yes, you would.
B Yes, but I think red cars are better.
C No, I haven't got one.

6 Jane: Do you go to school in the car?

Vicky: A No, I walk.
B No, I didn't.
C Yes, it's my school.

Movers practice test

Listen and tick (✓) the box. There is one example. 🔊41

Where did Paul and his mother go on Saturday?

A
B
C

1 What did they buy?

A
B
C

2 Where did Paul see the clown?

A
B
C

3 What did the clown do?

A
B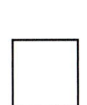
C

4 How did they go home?

A
B
C

Words

1 **Write the words.**

> cheese   chicken   milk   ~~pasta~~   coffee   salad   tea
> water   soup   sandwiches   vegetables   noodles

I'm hungry!

1	_pasta_	7	_____
2	_____	8	_____
3	_____	9	_____
4	_____	10	_____
5	_____	11	_____
6	_____	12	_____

2 **Look at the picture in Activity 1 and draw lines.**

The man has got   a **bowl**   of tea.

The girl has got   a **glass**   of water.

The woman has got   a **bottle**   of soup.

The boy has got   a **cup**   of pasta.

There is   a **plate**   of orange juice.

UNIT 8 WORDS   page 116

Reading & speaking

1 **Add more words and draw pictures.**

drinks	meat	other food
juice	burger	bread
fruit	**vegetables**	
pineapple	carrots	

2 **Complete the definitions. Then answer the questions.**

1 You make this with b_____. You can put cheese, meat or salad in it. What is it?   It's a _____.

2 This v_____ is long and orange. You can eat it in salads. What is it?   It's a _____.

3 This is a hot d_____, but it isn't tea. People often put milk in it. What is it?   It's _____.

4 You can buy water or j_____ in this. It isn't a cup or a glass. What is it?   It's a _____.

3 🎤 **Listen and circle.** 🔊42 **Ask and answer.**

1 What did you have for breakfast today?

2 Which drinks do you like best?

3 What's your favourite vegetable?

 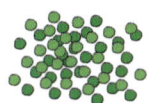

Story

1 Listen and read. Then act. 🔊43

1

Do you want to go to the playground?

I can't. I have to make the lunch.

2

I'm hungry! How much food have you got?

We've got lots! Would you like to come here for lunch?

Yes, please!

3

Hello, I'm here. I'm hot! And I'm very thirsty!

Hi, Jack! Put these on the table, please. Now, I think we've got some lemonade ... Oh, where is it?

4

It's here. It's very nice!

Oh, Jack. That's our lunch!

Sorry. I couldn't wait!

2 Write *a*, *an* or *some*. Then answer the question.

1 I've got __an__ apple.

2 I've got _____ lemons.

3 I've got _____ lemonade.

4 I've got _____ sandwich.

5 I've got _____ chocolate.

6 I've got _____ sausages.

Look at the nouns with *some*. Which ones are uncountable?

_____ and _____

GRAMMAR Countable and uncountable nouns page 120

Language practice

1 **Circle five differences. Complete the sentences.**

presents   juice   ~~cakes~~   chocolate   sandwiches

In picture 1, there are six (**1**) _____ cakes _____, and there are lots of
(**2**) _____. There is some (**3**) _____. There isn't
any (**4**) _____, and there aren't any (**5**) _____.

2 **Write about picture 2. Use the words from Activity 1.**

There are _____

_____

_____

3 **Look and complete the questions.**

1 How much __water__ have they got?   Only one bottle.

2 How many _____ have they got?   Six.

3 How much _____ have they got?   Lots!

4 How many _____ have they got?   Only two.

Language practice

1 **What does Jack have to do at home? Listen and tick (✓) or cross (✗).** 🔊44

clean bedroom	✓	clean the windows	☐
take the dog for a walk	✗	wash the car	☐
do the shopping	☐	eat fruit and vegetables	☐
cook the dinner	☐	do homework	☐

2 **Do the speaking activity.** P 130

Do you have to clean your bedroom?

Do you have to wash the car?

Yes, I do.

No, I don't.

3 **What do they have to do? Write.**

feed   sit   ~~say~~
water   carry   go

on the floor   a big bag   outside
the plants   the fish   ~~the alphabet~~

1 The children have to
say the alphabet.

2 The boy has to
_____

3 The children _____
_____

4 The girl
_____

5 The children _____
_____

6 The children _____
_____

Movers practice test

Look and read. Choose the correct words and write them on the lines.

a horse

ice cream

a tiger

a garden

cheese

a kitchen

pancakes

a duck

Example

This animal can run quickly. It lives in hot places
and it eats meat.   _____*a tiger*_____

Questions

1 This place is outside, next to your house.
   Children often play in it.   _____

2 You can see this animal at a farm.
   Some people like riding it.   _____

3 People often eat this food in sandwiches.
   It can be yellow, white or orange.   _____

4 This is a room in a house. You can cook
   dinner here. People sometimes eat here too.   _____

5 This food is very cold. You can eat it from
   a bowl.   _____

Listen and write. There is one example.

My birthday party

When?	on _____Monday_____

1   House number: _____

2   Street: _____ Street

3   Food: sandwiches, and
_____

4   How many children?   _____

5   Grown-ups: Mum, Dad and
_____

Movers practice test

Read the story. Choose a word from the box. Write the correct words next to numbers 1–5. There is one example.

My name is Lucy. Yesterday I went to the _____library_____ because I wanted to read some books. At twelve o'clock, my mum (**1**) _____ me. She wanted me to go home. 'I've got to go to the supermarket to buy some milk and fruit,' she said. I (**2**) _____ home quickly. My little brother was in the living room. I gave him a (**3**) _____ of water because he was thirsty. Then he asked me to make him a sandwich. I made two sandwiches and we ate them on the (**4**) _____ because it was a sunny day. We looked down and we could see a girl in the street. She had a ball. She shouted, 'Do you want to play?' We went (**5**) _____ and played football with her. She was a brilliant football player!

Example

library	ran	glass	downstairs

balcony	laughed	house	phoned

(6) Now choose the best name for the story. Tick (✓) one box.

A day at the library ☐

The girl who ran out of the library ☐

Lucy's busy day ☐

Revision 2

1 **Read and draw.**

The farmer has got a big brown moustache. He is drinking a cup of tea in his tractor.

The clown is carrying a bottle of water on his nose! He has got purple, curly hair.

The pirate can see an island on his map. There is some treasure in the box next to his feet.

The bus driver has got a blue hat. He is giving a boy a ticket.

2 **Listen and complete the question. ◀))46**
Then write and draw your answer.

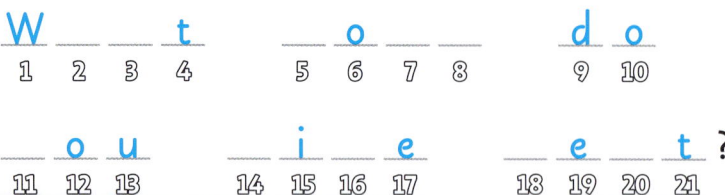

W ___ ___ t ___ ___ o ___ ___ d o
1 2 3 4   5 6 7 8   9 10

___ o u ___ ___ i e ___ ___ e ___ t ?
11 12 13   14 15 16 17   18 19 20 21

My answer: _____

3 Look, find the people and circle the correct words.

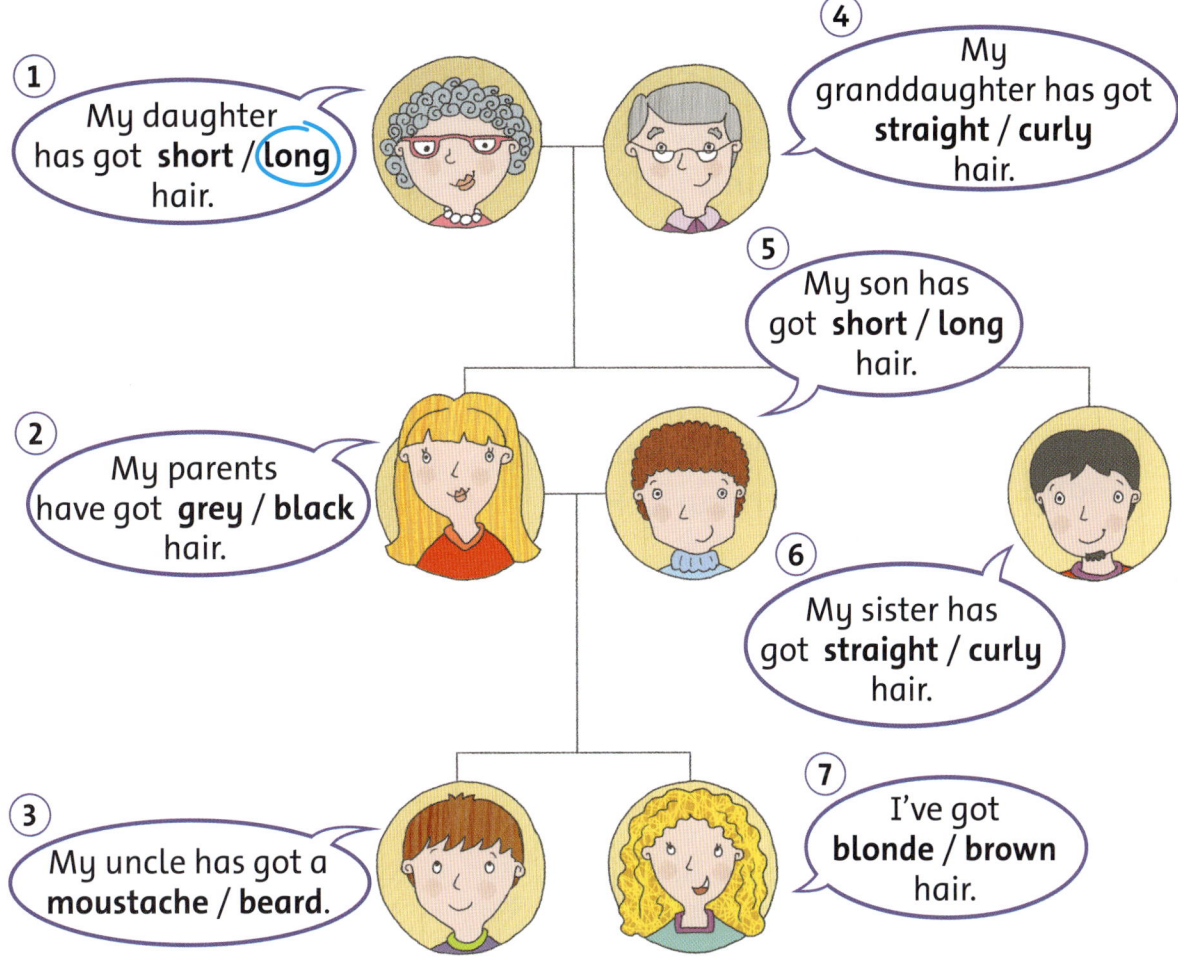

① My daughter has got **short / long** hair.

④ My granddaughter has got **straight / curly** hair.

⑤ My son has got **short / long** hair.

② My parents have got **grey / black** hair.

⑥ My sister has got **straight / curly** hair.

③ My uncle has got a **moustache / beard**.

⑦ I've got **blonde / brown** hair.

4 Write about three people in your family. Use the box to help you.

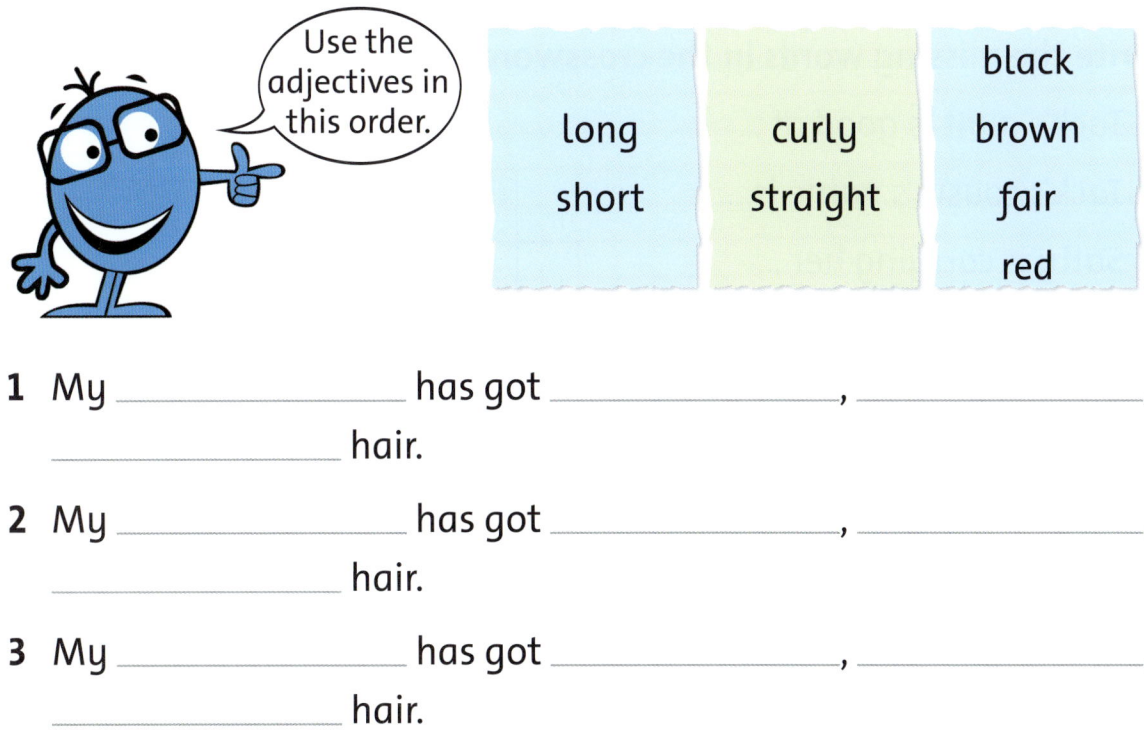

Use the adjectives in this order.

| long short | curly straight | black brown fair red |

1 My _____ has got _____, _____, _____ hair.

2 My _____ has got _____, _____, _____ hair.

3 My _____ has got _____, _____, _____ hair.

5 **Read about Jack's family. Draw lines.**

1 This is a photo of Zoe, who's very good at swimming. She's my aunt. This is her in her favourite swimming pool. She's wearing a green hat and a swimsuit.

2 Julia is my grandmother. She's a dentist. This is a photo of her in the place where she works. She's wearing a white coat and she's got brown curly hair.

3 My cousin Sally loves going for a walk at the weekend. In this photo she's wearing a white scarf and a blue jacket. She's carrying her lunch in a bag.

4 My mum's name is Vicky. She goes to the cinema every week. In this photo she is outside the cinema with her friends. She is wearing her new red coat.

a

b

c

d

6 **Write the missing words in the crossword. Then answer the question.**

1 Jack's aunt is good at ...

2 Jack's cousin's name is ...

3 Sally is carrying her ...

4 Jack's grandmother is a ...

5 Vicky goes to the cinema every ...

6 Sally's scarf is ...

7 Jack's mum has got a new ...

8 Julia has got curly ...

| 1 s | w | i | m | m | i | n | g |

What has Sally got in her bag?   A _____.

1 Circle five differences and complete the sentences. Listen and check. 🔊47

In Picture A, there's
a ____park____ ,

but in Picture B, there's a
_____ .

Here, there are _____ cars,

but here, there are _____ .

In this picture the boy is _____ ,

but in this one he's _____ .

Here, the woman has got a
_____ ,

but here, she's got some
_____ .

This door is _____ ,

but this one is _____ .

2 Circle the odd one out and complete the sentences.
Listen and check. 🔊48

These are all ____clothes____ ,
but this isn't.

In these pictures they're all
_____ . In this one
they're _____ .

These are all _____ ,
but this isn't.

These are all _____
the cupboard, but this is
_____ it.

SPEAKING TEST P 117 and 118

9 Do you like animals?

Words

1 Complete the words with double letters. Circle the animals that can be pets.

kangar o o   ki ___ en   pa ___ ot   pu ___ y

ra ___ it   gira ___ e   hi ___ o

2 Find, circle and write nine more animal words.

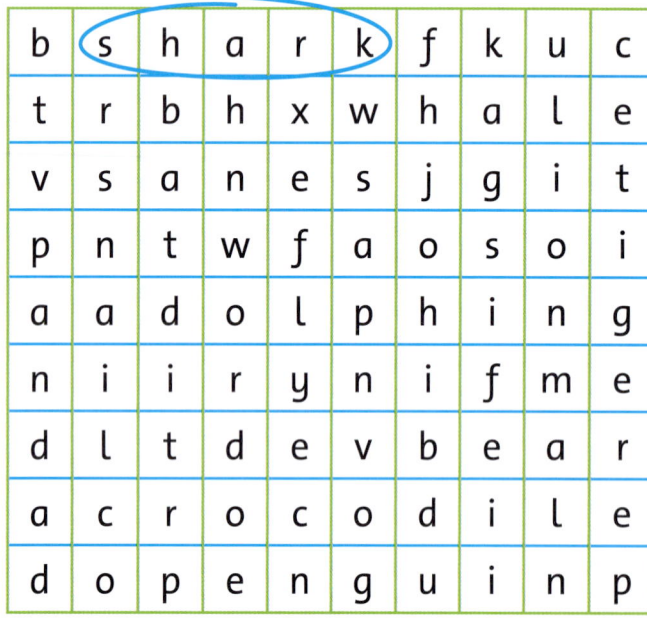

b	s	h	a	r	k	f	k	u	c
t	r	b	h	x	w	h	a	l	e
v	s	a	n	e	s	j	g	i	t
p	n	t	w	f	a	o	s	o	i
a	a	d	o	l	p	h	i	n	g
n	i	i	r	y	n	i	f	m	e
d	l	t	d	e	v	b	e	a	r
a	c	r	o	c	o	d	i	l	e
d	o	p	e	n	g	u	i	n	p

Across →

shark

Down ↓

Reading & speaking

1 **Read and circle *right* or *wrong*. Listen and check.** 🔊49

1	Pandas eat meat.	right	~~wrong~~
2	All sharks have got teeth.	right	wrong
3	Most crocodiles live in the sea.	right	wrong
4	A lion is a kind of cat.	right	wrong
5	A fly has got eight legs.	right	wrong
6	Crocodiles can run more quickly than hippos.	right	wrong
7	Bats can't stand up.	right	wrong
8	The biggest whale is bigger than a bus.	right	wrong
9	Hippos eat plants and fish.	right	wrong
10	The giraffe is the tallest animal in the world.	right	wrong

2 **Look and complete the sentences. Write one word on each line.**

1 The first giraffe is ___smaller___ .

2 The second puppy has got a bigger _____.

3 The first _____ has got a _____ tail.

4 The _____ _____ is bigger.

5 The _____ rabbit has got shorter _____.

3 🎤 **Listen and circle.** 🔊50 **Ask and answer.**

1 Have you got any pets?   yes    yes    no

2 Are you frightened of spiders?   yes   no

3 What's your favourite animal?

Story

1 **Listen and read. Then act.** 🔊 51

2 **Draw lines and write *must* or *mustn't*.**

You _____ put your fish in the water!

You _____ put your parrot in the bath!

You _____ give your rabbits a drink!

You **mustn't** open the cage.

You _____ feed the lions!

Language practice

1 **Read the words in the box.**
Listen and number the pictures.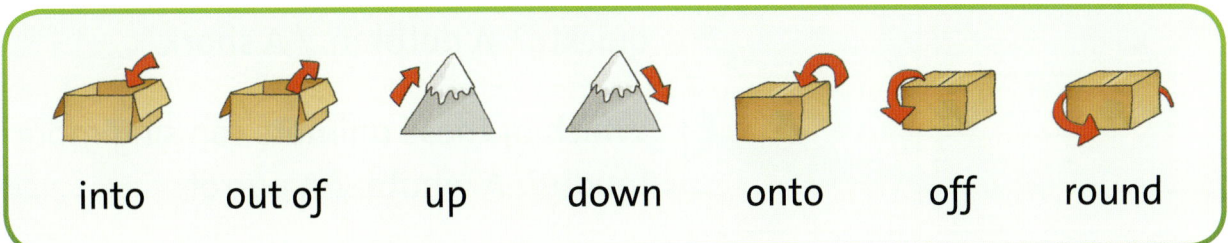

into   out of   up   down   onto   off   round

a   b   `1`   c   d

2 **Read and draw the parrot's route.**

My parrot jumped out of its cage, and it jumped onto the table. Then it flew off the table and flew up the stairs. It flew round my dad. Then it flew down the stairs, and it flew into its cage!

Language practice

1 **Guess the answers and circle. Listen and check.** 🔊 53

Which of these animals can swim more quickly? A dolphin. / A shark.

Which of these animals can sing more loudly? A whale. / A parrot.

Which of these animals can run more quickly? A giraffe. / A horse.

2 **Look, read and draw lines.**

 1. Why is Paul going into the bat house?

 2. Why has Clare got a fish?

 3. Why is Nick buying a burger?

 4. Why is Grace looking at the big cage?

 5. Why is Charlie surprised?

a. Because the elephant has got his ice cream.

b. Because he's hungry.

c. Because there are lots of parrots in it.

d. Because he loves little animals.

e. Because she wants to give it to the bear.

3 **Do the speaking activity.** P 131

Why is she opening the window? Because she's thirsty.

That's wrong! My turn.

UNIT 9 **WORDS** page 116

Movers practice test

Listen and draw lines. There is one example. 🔊54

Jane   Charlie   Lily   Fred

Mary   Peter   Jim

Movers practice test

Read the text. Choose the right words and write them on the lines.

Homes

Example There are lots of different kinds _____ of _____ homes. Some people live in houses and some people live in

1 flats. Most houses have two floors, _____ they can have three or four. A floor under the ground

2 _____ called a 'basement'. Often there is a

3 garden behind the house, _____ children can play. Lots of people who live in flats don't have gardens, but many flats have got balconies.

4 You _____ sit on the balcony and eat

5 _____ dinner there, or you can read a book.

Example	of	to	in
1	that	but	because
2	do	are	is
3	who	what	where
4	can	are	have
5	any	your	their

Movers practice test

Listen and colour and write. There is one example. 🔊 55

10 The weather

Words

1 **Write the words.**

| wind sun snow rain moon |
| rainbow stars ~~cloud~~ ice |

1 _____ cloud _____
2 _____
3 _____
4 _____
5 _____
6 _____
7 _____
8 _____
9 _____

2 **What's the weather like? Complete the sentences.**

| cold ~~hot~~ raining snowing windy cloudy sunny |

1 It's _ hot _ and _____.

2 It's _____.

3 It's _____.

4 It's _____.

5 It's _____.

6 It's _____.

Reading & speaking

1 **Look, listen and draw lines.** 🔊56

Monday   Tuesday   Wednesday   Thursday   Friday

1   2   3   4   5

2 **Read and draw the symbols.**

What was the weather like at the weekend?

On Saturday morning it was sunny. Then it was cloudy in the afternoon, but in the evening it was sunny again. On Sunday morning it rained, and in the afternoon it snowed! On Sunday evening it was cold, but it didn't snow.

	morning	afternoon	evening
Saturday			
Sunday			

3 🎤 **Listen and circle.** 🔊57 **Ask and answer.**

1 What's the weather like today?

2 Does it often snow in your country?

3 What do you wear when it's cold?

yes   no

Story

1 **Listen and read. Then act.** 🔊58

1. I went for a walk yesterday with my dad.

I don't like going for walks. They're boring!

2. Our walk was exciting!

Why? What was the weather like? Was it very windy?

No, but it was cold. I had to put on a coat and a scarf.

3. What did you see?

We saw some bats ... and we saw lots of stars, because there weren't any clouds.

4. You went for a walk at night? Wow! I like being outside at night!

So do I. It's better than going for a walk in the afternoon!

2 **Write *in*, *on* or *at*.**

1. Daisy went for a walk ____on____ Saturday evening.
She often goes for a walk _____ the weekend.

2. Jack often reads _____ the afternoon.
Sometimes he reads _____ night, too.

3. Daisy doesn't like eating cake _____ lunchtime.
But she loves eating it _____ her birthday!

4. Jack watched a film _____ Friday afternoon,
but he didn't watch TV _____ the evening.

GRAMMAR Prepositions of time page 120

UNIT 10 WORDS page 117

Language practice

1 **Read and complete the answers.**

1 What did Jack put on?

2 What did Daisy put in her bag?

3 What did Daisy take off?

4 What did Jack take to the park?

5 What did Daisy bring to the beach?

He put on his __shoes__.

She put a _____ in her bag.

She took off her _____.

He took his _____.

She brought a _____.

2 **Look and write the days.**

Tuesday

Thursday

Friday

Saturday

1 When did Jack see a lizard?
On ____Thursday____.

2 When did it snow?
On _____.

3 When did Daisy play hockey?
On _____.

4 When did Daisy paint her
bedroom? On _____.

5 When did Daisy go to Jack's
house? On _____.

6 When did Jack wear his red hat?
On _____.

7 When did it rain?
On _____.

8 When did Jack fix his model?
On _____.

3 **Cut out the cards. Then play the game.** **P** 132

When did you go shopping?

In the afternoon?

In the morning?

On Saturday.

No.

Yes.

Language practice

1 **Write two verbs for each noun.**

> ~~drive~~   take off   ask   put on   make   catch   answer   cook

_____drive_____ a bus
_____ a bus

_____ a question
_____ a question

_____ dinner
_____ dinner

_____ your clothes
_____ your clothes

2 **Circle the correct noun.**

They're having a **party** / **drink**.

She's having a **picnic** / **dream**.

He's having a **holiday** / **shower**.

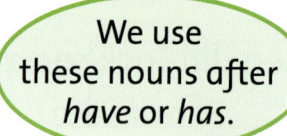
We use these nouns after _have_ or _has_.

3 **Write the nouns from Activity 2.**

1 I'm having a _____drink_____ because I'm thirsty.

2 We had a _____ last year. We went to the beach every day!

3 I have a _____ in the evenings because we haven't got a bath.

4 We couldn't have a _____ on Saturday because it rained.

5 Last night I had a bad _____ and I was frightened.

6 I had a _____ yesterday because it was my birthday.

Movers practice test

Look and read and write.

Examples

The man with a bottle of water has got a brown _____ beard _____.

What is the man with fair hair eating? _____ a banana _____

Complete the sentences.

1   On the girl's jacket, there's a picture of a _____.

2   The brown duck is smaller than the white _____.

Answer the questions.

3   Where are the flowers?

_____

4   How many people are there?

_____

Now write two sentences about the picture.

5   _____

6   _____

Movers practice test

Mr Walker is telling Sue about his family and friends and what they did on Saturday afternoon. What did each person do?

Listen and write a letter in each box. There is one example. 🔊59

Mr Walker — **F**

Mrs Walker — ☐

Paul — ☐

Vicky — ☐

Fred — ☐

Mary — ☐

A

B

C

D

E

F

G

H

Movers practice test

Look at the pictures and read the story. Write some words to complete the sentences about the story. You can use 1, 2 or 3 words. There are two examples

The bike ride

Jim lives in a city with his parents and his sister. Last Sunday it was sunny and hot. 'Let's go for a bike ride,' Jim's dad said. They drove to the beach, then they rode their bikes by the sea. Jim loved the ride, but he was hot and thirsty. He wanted to have a drink. They stopped at a café for lunch. Jim had some orange juice. His mother bought him pancakes with chocolate sauce but he didn't eat them. 'I'm not hungry,' he said.

Examples

Jim and his family live _____ in a city _____.

Jim's dad wanted to go for _____ a bike ride _____.

Questions

1 They rode their bikes next to _____.

2 Jim drank _____ in the café.

3 He didn't eat the _____ that his mother bought.

In the afternoon, they rode their bikes again. Jim could see lots of black clouds. Then it started to rain. Jim looked in his bag, but his jacket wasn't there. They rode home quickly and went inside. When they were inside, Jim took off his sweater. It was very wet! He went upstairs and had a shower, then he put on a T-shirt.

4 Jim's _____ wasn't in his bag.

5 Jim took off his sweater because it was _____!

6 Jim put on _____ after his shower.

11 What's the matter?

Words

I feel ill!

1 Write the words. Then add more body words.

> arm   shoulder   stomach   leg   foot
> head   teeth   neck   back   hand

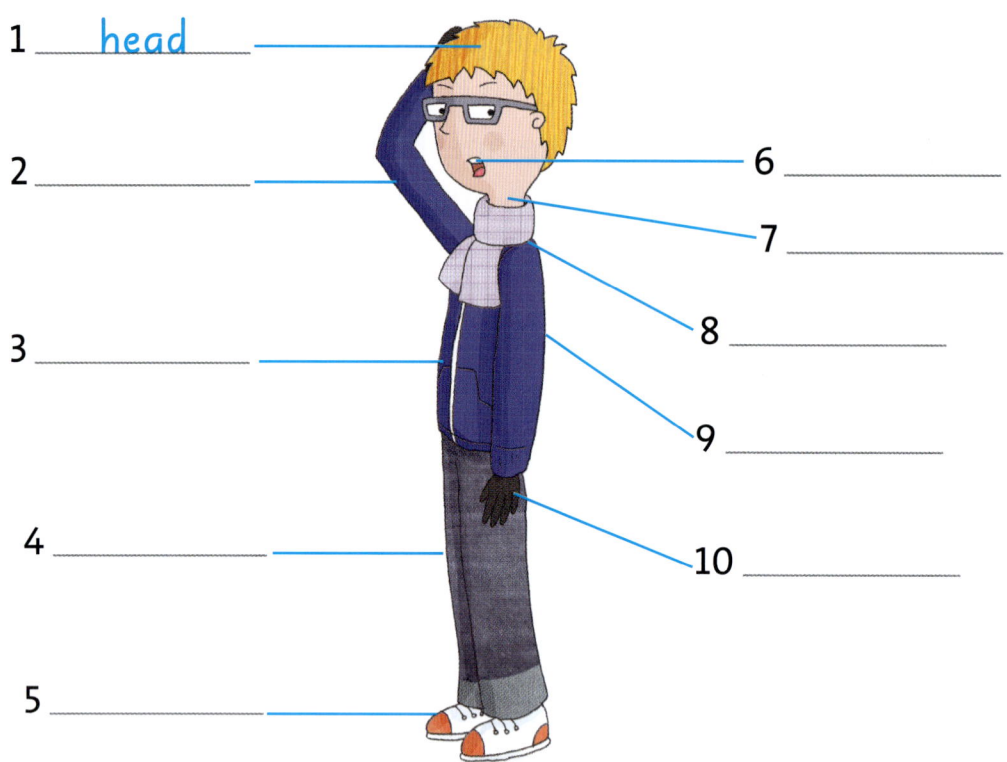

1 head

2 _____

3 _____

4 _____

5 _____

6 _____

7 _____

8 _____

9 _____

10 _____

2 What are they saying? Circle.

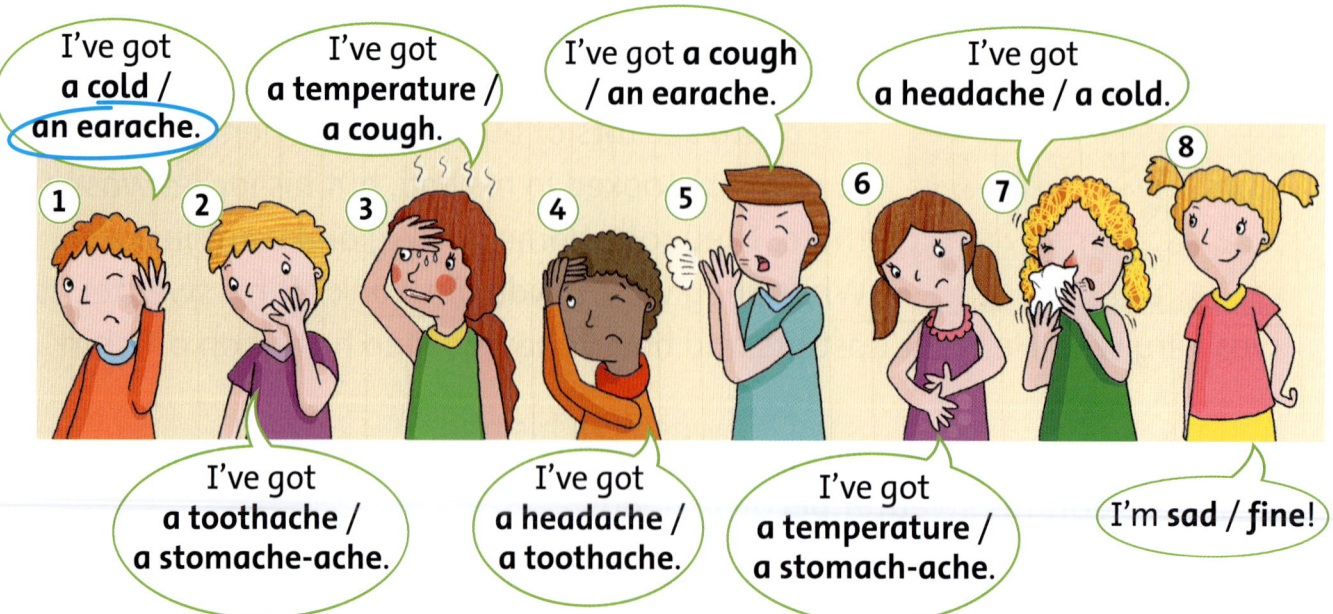

I've got **a cold** / **an earache.**

I've got **a temperature** / **a cough.**

I've got **a cough** / **an earache.**

I've got **a headache** / **a cold.**

I've got **a toothache** / **a stomache-ache.**

I've got **a headache** / **a toothache.**

I've got **a temperature** / **a stomach-ache.**

I'm **sad** / **fine!**

UNIT 11
WORDS   page 117

Reading & speaking

1 Choose words from Activity 2 on page 92 and complete the dialogue. Then act.

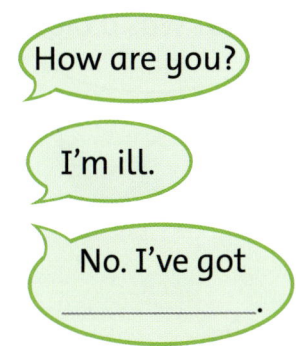 How are you?

I'm ill.

No. I've got _____.

I'm fine, thank you. How are you?

What's the matter? Have you got _____?

2 Write the irregular plurals.

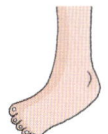  

one foot   two ___feet___   one tooth   lots of _____

one child   two _____   one fish   lots of _____

one man   three _____   one sheep   two _____

one woman   two _____

3 Look, read and write the letters.

1   C

2

3

4

a His arms hurt.   **b** His ear hurts.   **c** His feet hurt.   **d** His back hurts.

4 🎤 Listen and circle. 🔊60 Ask and answer.

1   What colour are your eyes?

2   Do you wear glasses?   yes   no

3   How many grown-up teeth have you got?   3   8   9   11

Story

1 Listen and read. Then act. 🔊61

2 Look at the pictures. Read the questions and answers. Then draw lines.

How about a drink?

What about going swimming?

How about taking a photo?

What about this dress?

How about buying some cakes?

Good idea. Smile!

All right. Those ones are my favourites.

OK, that's a great idea. I'm hot!

No, thanks. I'm not thirsty.

Sorry, I don't like that colour.

GRAMMAR *How / What about ...?* page 119

UNIT 11 WORDS page 117

Language practice

1 **What do they need to do? Write.**

~~drink~~ put on eat go see	to bed his lunch the doctor ~~some water~~ a different sweater

 He's got a headache. _He needs to drink some water_ .

 They're tired. _They need to_ _____._

 He feels sick. _____.

 She's wet. _____.

 He's hungry. _____.

2 **Look at the pictures and answer the questions.**

 What do you need when you do your homework?
   You need a pencil but you don't need ice skates .

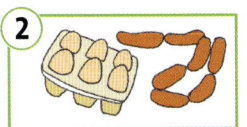 What do you need when you make a cake?
   You need _____.

 What do you need when you have a shower?
   _____.

 What do you need when you clean your teeth?
   _____.

3 **Cut out the cards and the shopping lists. Then play the game.** P 133

Who needs eggs?
Here you are.

I do.
Thank you.

Language practice

1 Colour the pairs of opposites. Circle the two adjectives that don't have an opposite.

dry quiet naughty fat strong short loud

clever thin ugly tall weak wet pretty

2 Complete. Listen, check and say the chant. 🔊62

Which cat is fatter, the [1] black one or the white one?

The white cat is fatter. Can't you see?

Which man is stronger, the [2] _____ one or the short one?

The short man is stronger. He's stronger than me!

Which dog is cleverer, the brown one or the [3] _____ one?

The brown dog is cleverer. Can't you see?

Which car is louder, the big one or the [4] _____ one?

The small car is louder. It's too loud for me!

Which tree is taller, the [5] _____ one or the red one?

The red tree is taller. Can't you see?

Which monkey's naughtier, the fat one or the [6] _____ one?

The fat monkey's naughtier. He's naughtier than me!

3 Complete the sentences.

1 The white ____cat____ is ____fatter____ than the black one.

2 The short _____ is _____ than the tall one.

3 The brown _____ is _____ than the grey one.

4 The small _____ is _____ than the big one.

Movers practice test

Listening, Part 2

Listen and write. There is one example. 🔊63

Morton Sports Centre

Day: _____Tuesday_____

1   Ages of children: _____

and _____

2   Ate: _____

3   Drank: _____

4   Favourite sport: _____

5   Name: Mrs _____

Movers practice test

Read the story. Choose a word from the box. Write the correct words next to numbers 1–5. There is one example.

My name is Charlie. Last night I had a dream. In my dream I went to school with my ___friends___, but it wasn't my school. It was different. When we walked into the (1)_____, the teacher wasn't there, but there were lots of animals. We (2) _____ next to the window and watched the animals. There was a very clever (3) _____ that wrote on the board! It taught us English! I looked outside and I saw a lion walking along the path. It looked dangerous! It ran inside and jumped onto a table. I wasn't very brave. I was frightened and I woke up. My (4) _____ woke up too, and she came into my bedroom. She gave me a glass of water. I (5) _____ it, then I wasn't frightened.

Example

friends	opened	classroom	stood
drank	mother	shouted	panda

(6) Now choose the best name for the story. Tick (✓) one box.

Some animals that Charlie likes ☐

A film about animals ☐

A dream about a different school ☐

Movers practice test

Listen and tick (✓) the box. There is one example. 🔊64

What was the matter with Fred yesterday?

A    B    C

1 Which doctor did he see at the hospital?

A    B    C

2 What did he have for dinner?

A    B    C

3 What present did his friend bring?

A    B    C

4 Who took Fred home?

A    B    C

12 In the countryside

Words

1 **Write the numbers.**

grass [6] river [ ] field [ ] waterfall [ ]

mountain [ ] farm [ ] lake [ ] forest [ ]

leaf [ ] rock [ ] road [ ] sky [ ]

I like the countryside.

2 **Look, read and draw lines.**

1	There are lots of leaves	**a**	at the top of the mountain.
2	There is grass	**b**	next to the river.
3	There is snow	**c**	in all the fields.
4	There are rocks	**d**	at the bottom of the waterfall.
5	There is a lorry	**e**	next to the farm.
6	There is a forest	**f**	on the trees in the forest.
7	There is a lake	**g**	on the road.

Reading & speaking

1 **Which things can you see in the picture on page 100? Tick (✓) or cross (✗).**

helicopter ✗ bike ☐ boat ☐ plane ☐ bus ☐

car ☐ train ☐ lorry ☐ motorbike ☐ tractor ☐

2 **Read and complete the picture. Follow the instructions.**

Draw a road between the farm and the lake.

Draw two men at the top of the mountain.

Draw a lorry on the road and colour it green.

Draw some rocks in front of the lake.

Draw two clouds in the sky and colour them grey.

Draw a forest behind the farm.

3 🎤 **Listen and circle.** 🔊65 **Ask and answer.**

1 Which do you like best, the town or the country?   town   country

2 Are there any mountains near your home?   yes   no

3 What do you do when you go to the countryside?

4 How do you travel to school?

Story

1 Listen and read. Then act. 🔊66

2 Read and write A or B.

1 There is **something** yellow on Daisy's hat. _A_

2 **Everyone** is carrying a bag. _____

3 Jack is talking to **someone**. _____

4 **Everything** on the table is green or yellow. _____

5 **No one** is wearing a coat. _____

6 There is **nothing** on Daisy's hat. _____

3 Write these words in your language.

everything _____   something _____   nothing _____

everyone _____   someone _____   no one _____

Language practice

1 Listen and write the numbers.  🔊67

Jack's trip to the countryside

2 Look at the pictures. Read the questions and circle *a* or *b*.

Picture 1: What did they do when it was sunny on Sunday?
    a They went for a walk by the river.
    (b) They went for a walk in the forest.

Picture 2: What did they do when they were hungry?
    a They had a picnic.   **b** They went into a café.

Picture 3: What did they do when it started to rain?
    a They put on their coats.   **b** They stood under a tree.

Picture 4: What did Jack do when the bird started to sing?
    a He took a photo.   **b** He started to sing.

Picture 5: What did they do when the rain stopped?
    a They walked up a mountain.   **b** They caught a bus.

Picture 6: What did they do when they were tired?
    a They walked home.   **b** They caught a bus.

3 Cover the text above and look at the pictures. Tell the story.

They went for a walk in the forest.

Then they...

GRAMMAR *when* clauses (past tense)

UNIT 12 WORDS page 118 Unit 12 **103**

Language practice

1 **Replace the red words with words that mean the same.**

> next to   Hello   ~~afraid~~   one more
> brown   Goodbye   blonde   your   under

1
Jump!

No, I don't want to. I'm ~~frightened~~! **afraid**

2
Which girl is your sister?

She's the one with **fair** hair.

3
Excuse me. Where's the library?

It's there, **by** the supermarket.

4
I've got to go home now.

OK. **See you**!

5
I'm hungry!

Would you like **another** cake?

2 **Ask and answer.**

What does *by* mean?

It means ...

3 **Do the speaking activity.** **P** 134

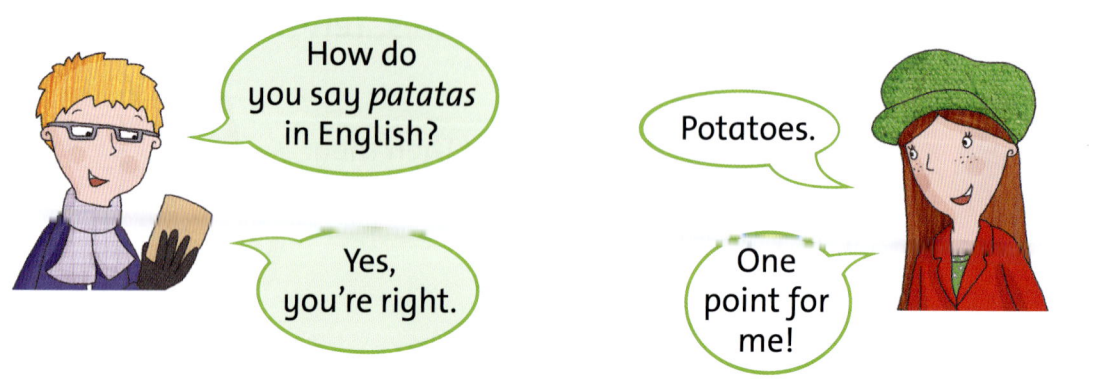

How do you say *patatas* in English?

Yes, you're right.

Potatoes.

One point for me!

Movers practice test

Look and read. Choose the correct words and write them on the lines.

a watermelon

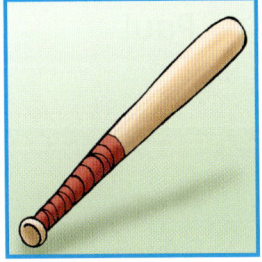

a bat

a lake

a tomato

a mountain

a field

a volleyball net

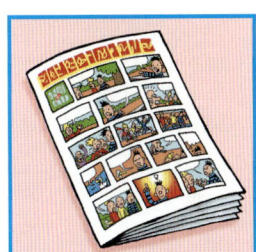

a comic

Examples

You can climb up this. Sometimes there is snow on the top of it.

_____ a mountain _____

Questions

1 You can play baseball with this. You need a ball too.

_____

2 This fruit is very big. The inside is red and the outside is green.

_____

3 This food is red. You can put it in salads and sandwiches.

_____

4 You can find this in the countryside. Sometimes there is grass in it.

_____

5 Children like reading this. It isn't a book. There are lots of pictures in it.

_____

Movers practice test

Listen and draw lines. There is one example. 🔊 68

Jane   Sally   Paul   Mary

Jim   Fred   Peter

Movers practice test

Reading & Writing, Part 2

Read the text and choose the best answer.

Paul is talking to his friend Julia.

Example

Julia: Hello, Paul! Whose bike is that?

Paul:
A   It's in the garden.
B   It's mine! It's new.
C   Yes, it is.

Questions

1 **Julia:** Can I ride with you?

  Paul:
A   All right.
B   No, it's with you.
C   Yes, you are.

2 **Julia:** Did you go to the park yesterday?

  Paul:
A   At the park.
B   Yes, it did.
C   Yes, I did.

3 **Julia:** What was the weather like?

  Paul:
A   Yes, I like it.
B   It's sunny.
C   It was cloudy.

4 **Julia:** How is your sister?

  Paul:
A   She's at the cinema.
B   She's fine.
C   She's got brown hair.

5 **Julia:** I'm thirsty! How much water have you got?

  Paul:
A   It's a bottle.
B   No, I haven't.
C   Lots! Here you are.

6 **Julia:** Do you want to come to my house?

  Paul:
A   Sorry, I've got to go home now.
B   Yes, I would.
C   No, it's my house.

Revision 3

1 **Write the animal words.**

> lion   panda   ~~bear~~   fly   puppy   bat   giraffe
> rabbit   parrot   whale   kangaroo   hippo   tiger

A (**1**) _____bear_____ is sleeping on the rocks. There is a (**2**) _____
on the (**3**) _____'s neck. A (**4**) _____ is swimming in
the lake. A (**5**) _____ is hiding in the grass. A (**6**) _____
is flying above the (**7**)_____. There is a (**8**) _____
in the tree.

2 **Think and write.**

Can you name:

three animals that live
in the sea?   _____   _____   _____

three kinds of fruit?   _____   _____   _____

three vegetables?   _____   _____   _____

three drinks?   _____   _____   _____

three places in a town?   _____   _____   _____

three things that you
can wear?   _____   _____   _____

three parts of your body?   _____   _____   _____

three kinds of weather?   _____   _____   _____

REVISION 3 WORDS   pages 112–120

3 Listen and number. Then listen again and write the names. 🔊69

Vicky   Jim   Jane   ~~Mary~~   Peter   Fred

1

_____   _____   ___Mary_____

4 Read the questions and answers. Draw lines.

1 Which child needs some food for her animals?   **a** Jane

2 Which child needs a glass?   **b** Peter

3 Which child needs to go home?   **c** Vicky

4 Which child needs a pen?   **d** Fred

5 Which child needs to put on a coat?   **e** Jim

6 Which child needs to buy a ticket?   **f** Mary

5 **Write the words and cross out the letters.**

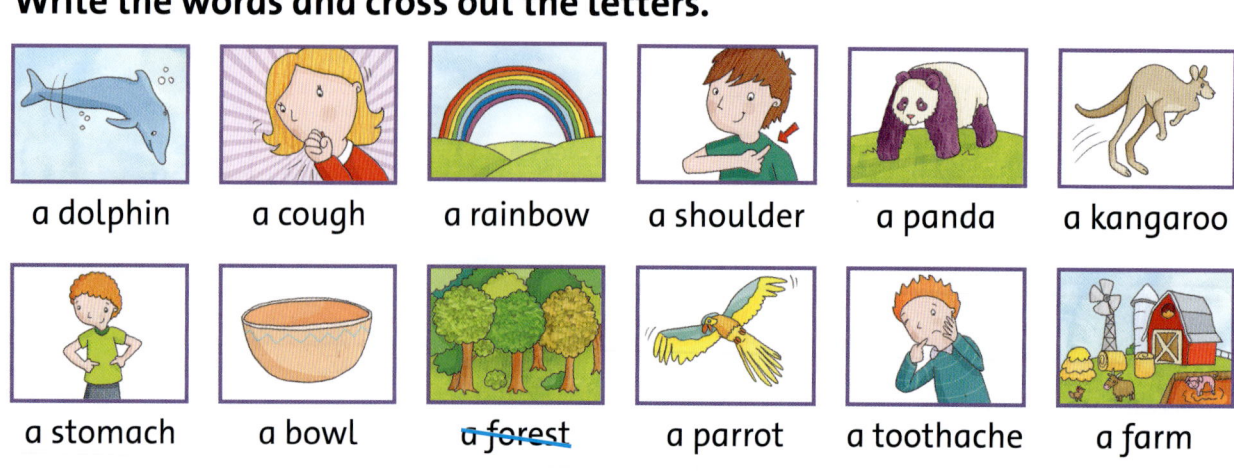

a dolphin a cough a rainbow a shoulder a panda a kangaroo

a stomach a bowl a ~~forest~~ a parrot a toothache a farm

1 You can find lots of trees in this place.
Sometimes you can go for a walk there.

a _____ forest _____
ⓦf̸ø̸ⓗⓐ̸¢̸ⓣ̸s̸t̸

2 When you have this, your teeth hurt.

a _____
t w o o t h a c a h e s

3 This is a part of your body. When you eat,
your food goes here.

a _____
t s t o h m a c e h

4 This black and white animal eats plants.
It is a kind of bear.

a _____
w e p a a n t d h e r a

5 This is an animal. It swims in the sea,
but it is not a fish.

a _____
l i d o l k p h e i n

6 This animal stands on two legs. It can't
run, but it can jump. It is bigger than a rabbit.

a _____
o k a n g a r o n o

7 We sometimes see this when it is sunny
and it rains. There are lots of colours in it.

a _____
y r a i o n b o u w r

8 You find this thing in a kitchen.
It is round and you can put soup in it.

a _____
b b i o r w t h d l a y

6 **Circle the letters that aren't crossed out and write the question.**
Then ask and answer.

The question is: __What_____

_____ ?

1 **Look at the pictures. Circle the words that you think will be in the story.**

sad   running   sunny   shop   sitting   closed   buying

living room   watching   kitchen   cinema   raining   DVD

2 **Listen and order the pictures in Activity 1.** 🔊70 **Tell the story.**

3 **Circle the odd one out. Complete the sentences and write the letters.**

1  These are ___ *water* ___,
but this is a _____.

2     These are _____,
but this isn't.

3     These are _____,
but this isn't.

4     In these pictures it's _____,
but in this one it's _____.

Wordlist

Abbreviations

The following abbreviations have been used where it is necessary to show the part of speech:

n = noun   v = verb   adj = adjective   pron = pronoun prep = preposition

Words marked with * are not on the Movers wordlist, but have been included for the sake of completeness.

Names

Boys: Charlie   Fred   Jack   Jim   Paul   Peter

Girls: Daisy   Jane   Lily   Mary   Sally   Vicky   Clare   Julia   Zoe

○ Where do you live?

address _____

basement _____

dress up _____

eighty _____

fifty _____

first _____

forty _____

fourth _____

ground floor _____

ninety _____

one hundred _____

second _____

seventy _____

sixty _____

third _____

thirty _____

① At the park

a pair of _____

all right _____

asleep _____

be good at _____

careful _____

carry _____

climb _____

coat _____

cry _____

dance _____

down _____

fall _____

fish (v) _____

help _____

hide _____

hop _____

laugh _____

roller skates _____

scarf _____

skip _____

sweater _____

swimsuit _____

tall _____

than _____

who (*pron*) _____

② A busy week

always _____

at (*prep. of time*) _____

call _____

CD _____

cook _____

drive (*n*) _____

DVD _____

e-book _____

email (*n, v*) _____

every _____

film (*US movie*) _____

Friday _____

go shopping _____

homework _____

How / What about ...?

_____

How often? _____

idea _____

internet _____

Monday _____

music _____

never _____

often _____

on _____

practice _____

ride (*n*) _____

sail _____

Saturday _____

Shall I ...? _____

sometimes _____

Sunday _____

swim (*n*) _____

text (*n, v*) _____

thing _____

Thursday _____

Tuesday _____

walk (*n*) _____

wash _____

website _____

Wednesday _____

week _____

weekend _____

When? _____

Who? _____

③ In the town

above (*prep*) _____

afraid _____

after _____

app _____

band (*e.g. rock band*)

_____

be called _____

below (*prep*) _____

bus station _____

busy _____

buy _____

café _____

car park _____

catch (*e.g. a bus*) _____

circus _____

cold _____

Excuse me. _____

funfair _____

hospital _____

hot _____

huge _____

last _____

library _____

market _____

near (*prep*) _____

opposite (*prep*) _____

pop star _____

practise _____

present _____

roof _____

shopping centre _____

sports centre _____

square _____

station _____

supermarket _____

surprised _____

then _____

tired _____

town centre _____

town _____

wet _____

when _____

Why ...? _____

yesterday _____

④ At home

any _____

around _____

bat _____

blanket _____

cage _____

comic (book) _____

dance (*v*) _____

downstairs _____

drop _____

get dressed _____

get up _____

ground _____

helmet _____

inside _____

laptop _____

look for _____

lose _____

map _____

outside _____

plant (*n, v*) _____

round (*adj*) _____

shop (*v*) _____

shout _____

shower _____

square (*adj*) _____

thing _____

think _____

toothbrush _____

toothpaste _____

towel _____

upstairs _____

wake (*up*) _____

world _____

⑤ Let's go on holiday!

awake _____

balcony _____

bus stop _____

cinema _____

get off _____

get on _____

get undressed _____

holiday _____

lift (*US elevator*) _____

message _____

milkshake _____

(*swimming*) pool _____

seat _____

send _____

stair(s) _____

ticket _____

wait _____

wave (*n*) _____

which (*pron*) _____

⑥ My favourite book

all _____

bad _____

because _____

best _____

better _____

boring _____

both _____

building _____

city _____

clown _____

cook (*n*) _____

difficult _____

doctor _____

driver _____

easy _____

exciting _____

famous _____

farm _____

farmer _____

goal _____

How ...? _____

invite _____

island _____

jungle _____

kind (*n*) _____

machine _____

mistake _____

more _____

most _____

nurse _____

pirate _____

place (*n*) _____

score (*v*) _____

terrible _____

treasure _____

video _____

village _____

work (*n, v*) _____

worse _____

worst _____

would _____

Would you like ...?

_____

⑦ This is my family

age _____

aunt _____

badly _____

beard _____

blond(e) _____

build (*v*) _____

circle _____

could (*past of 'can'*)

_____

curly _____

daughter _____

fair _____

granddaughter _____

grandparent _____

grandson _____

grow (*v*) _____

grown-up _____

loud _____

loudly _____

model _____

moustache _____

parent _____

quick _____

quickly _____

quiet _____

quietly _____

slow _____

slowly _____

son _____

straight _____

uncle _____

well (*adv*) _____

⑧ What's for lunch?

before _____

bottle _____

bowl _____

break e.g. lunch break

_____

cheese _____

coffee _____

cup _____

feed (*v*) _____

glass _____

have (got) to _____

how much _____

hungry _____

little _____

noodles _____

only _____

pancake _____

party _____

pasta _____

plate _____

player _____

salad _____

sandwich _____

soup _____

tea _____

thirsty _____

vegetable _____

water (*v*) _____

9 Do you like animals?

bat _____

bear _____

change (v) _____

difference _____

dolphin _____

fly _____

frightened _____

into _____

kangaroo _____

kitten _____

lion _____

must _____

noise _____

off _____

onto* _____

out of _____

panda _____

parrot _____

penguin _____

pet _____

puppy _____

rabbit _____

round _____

shark _____

snail _____

up _____

whale _____

wrong _____

10 The weather

bring _____

cloud _____

cloudy _____

dream _____

film star _____

fix _____

holiday _____

ice _____

in _____

moon _____

picnic _____

put on _____

rain (n, v) _____

rainbow _____

snow (n, v) _____

star _____

sunny _____

take _____

take off _____

weather _____

What is / was the weather like?

_____

wind _____

windy _____

11 What's the matter?

all right (adj) _____

along _____

back _____

brave _____

clever _____

cold (n) _____

cough _____

dangerous _____

different _____

dry _____

earache _____

fat _____

fine _____

headache _____

hurt _____

ice skates _____

ill _____

kick (*n*) _____

naughty _____

neck _____

need _____

pretty _____

shoulder _____

sick _____

stomach-ache _____

stomach _____

strong _____

teach (*v*) _____

temperature _____

thin _____

tooth / teeth _____

toothache _____

weak _____

well _____

What's the matter?

_____

(12) In the countryside

another _____

bottom _____

by _____

carefully _____

centre _____

Come on! _____

country(side) _____

everyone _____

everything _____

field _____

forest _____

grass _____

lake _____

leaf / leaves _____

mean (*v*) _____

mountain _____

move _____

net _____

no one* _____

nothing _____

river _____

road _____

rock _____

safe _____

See you! _____

sky _____

someone _____

something _____

sweet (*adj*) _____

top _____

tractor _____

travel _____

trip _____

waterfall _____

Grammar

be good at

be good at + noun	My parents **are good at** English.	She **isn't good at** sport.
be good at + verb + **ing**	That boy **is good at** dancing.	They **aren't good at** fishing.

Comparative and superlative adjectives

	adjective	comparative adjective	superlative adjective
Short	long big pretty	long**er** bigg**er** pretti**er**	long**est** bigg**est** pretti**est**
Long	exciting famous	**more** exciting **more** famous	**most** exciting **most** famous
Irregular	**good** **bad**	**better** **worse**	**best** **worst**

Relative clauses

People	Can you find a boy **who** is skipping?
Things	Can you see a tree **that** has got flowers?
Places	This is the café **where** we had breakfast.

Shall I …?

Offers		Suggestions	
Shall I open the window?	Yes, please. I'm hot!	**Shall I write** a story?	Yes, good idea.
Shall I make dinner?	No, thanks. I'm not hungry.	**Shall I swim** in the sea?	No! It's too cold!

How / What about …?

How/What about + noun ?	How about you?	What about this one?
How/What about + verb + ing ?	How about going swimming?	What about taking a photo?

The past simple

For other irregular verbs, see the list on page 121.

	Regular verbs	Irregular verbs
+	She **watched** a film.	I **went** shopping yesterday.
–	They **didn't watch** television.	I **didn't go** to school.
?	What film **did** she **watch**? **Did** you **watch** a DVD on Saturday?	When **did** you **go** to the shops? **Did** he **go** for a swim yesterday?
Short answers	Yes, we **did**.	No, he **didn't**.

The past simple (*was / were*)

	I/He/She was …	You/We/They were …
+	I **was** happy.	We **were** hungry.
–	She **wasn't** in the park.	We **weren't** at school.
?	Why **was** she sad? **Was** he in the kitchen?	Where **were** your parents yesterday? **Were** they at home?
Short answers	Yes, he **was**.	No, they **weren't**.

Verbs with indirect objects

The girl **bought** an ice cream **for Daisy.**	→ The girl **bought Daisy** an ice cream.
Daisy **is writing** an email **to Jack.**	→ Daisy is **writing Jack** an email.

ask / want / invite someone to do something

	want	ask / invite
+	I **want** you **to draw** a picture. He **wants** Charlie **to close** the window.	Paul **is asking** Grace **to make** a cake. Lily **is inviting** Dan **to go** to the park.

could / couldn't

+	I **could swim** when I was three.
–	Jack's sister **couldn't see** Daisy.
?	**Could** you **write** when you were five?
Short answers	Yes, I **could**. No, I **couldn't**.

Countable and uncountable nouns

	Countable nouns		Uncountable nouns
	one	more than one	
+	There's **a** lemon.	She's got **some** lemons.	There is **some** lemonade.
–	He hasn't got **a** lemon.	There aren't **any** lemons.	We haven't got **any** lemonade.
?	Have we got **a** lemon?	Has he got **any** lemons? **How many** lemons are there?	Is there **any** lemonade? **How much** lemonade have we got?

some, any, How much / many...?

+	There **are some** sandwiches.	
–	There **aren't any** apples.	
?	**Are** there **any** lemons?	
much	How **much water** have you got?	I've got lots of water!
many	How **many bananas** have you got?	I've got three bananas.

have/has (got) to for obligation

	have to	have got to	had to (past)
+	I **have to** clean my room.	I **have got to** clean my room.	I **had to clean** my room.
–	She **doesn't have to** go home.	She **hasn't got to** go home.	She **didn't have to** go home.
?	**Do** they **have to** eat fruit?	**Have** they **got to** eat fruit?	**Did** they **have to** eat fruit?
Short answers	Yes, they **do**. No, they **don't**.	Yes, they **have**. No, they **haven't**.	Yes, they **did**. No, they **didn't**.

must

+	You **must put** your fish in the water!
–	We **mustn't ride** our bikes here.
?	**Must** we **go** to bed now?

Prepositions of time

in (periods of time)	on (days and dates)	at (specific times)	last (recent past)	this (today)
in the morning **in** the afternoon **in** the evening	**on** Sunday **on** Wednesdays **on** Tuesday morning **on** my birthday	**at** the weekend **at** lunchtime **at** night	**last** night **last** week **last** weekend	**this** morning **this** afternoon **this** evening

need

	need + noun	need + to + infinitive
+	She **needs** a drink.	I **need** to do my homework.
–	We **don't need** our bags.	He **doesn't need to change** his clothes.
?	**Do** you **need** a pencil?	**Does** he **need** to get up now?
Short answers	Yes, I **do**. No, I **don't**.	Yes, he **does**. No, he **doesn't**.